REPRESENTATIVE GOVERNMENT
IN SOUTHEAST ASIA

THE INSTITUTE OF PACIFIC RELATIONS

The Institute of Pacific Relations is an unofficial and non-partisan organization, founded in 1925 to facilitate the scientific study of the peoples of the Pacific area. It is composed of autonomous National Councils in the principal countries having important interests in the Pacific area, together with an International Secretariat. It is privately financed by contributions from National Councils, corporations and foundations. It is governed by a Pacific Council composed of members appointed by each of the National Councils.

In addition to the independent activities of its National Councils, the Institute organizes private international conferences every two or three years. Such conferences have been held at Honolulu (1925 & 1927), Kyoto (1929), Shanghai (1931), Banff, Canada (1933), Yosemite Park, California (1936), Virginia Beach, Virginia (1939), Mont Tremblant, Quebec (1942), Hot Springs, Virginia (1945), Stratford, England (1947), Lucknow, India (1950) and Kyoto (1954). The Institute conducts an extensive program of research on the political, economic and social problems of the Pacific area and the Far East. It also publishes the proceedings of its conferences, a quarterly journal, *Pacific Affairs*, and a large number of scholarly books embodying the results of its studies.

Neither the International Secretariat nor the National Councils of the Institute advocate policies or express opinions on national or international affairs. Responsibility for statements of fact or opinion in Institute publications rests solely with the authors.

NATIONAL COUNCILS

AMERICAN INSTITUTE OF PACIFIC RELATIONS, INC.
AUSTRALIAN INSTITUTE OF INTERNATIONAL AFFAIRS
CANADIAN INSTITUTE OF INTERNATIONAL AFFAIRS
COMITE D'ETUDES DES PROBLEMS DU PACIFIQUE
INDIAN COUNCIL OF WORLD AFFAIRS
INDONESIAN INSTITUTE OF WORLD AFFAIRS
JAPAN INSTITUTE OF PACIFIC RELATIONS
NETHERLANDS COUNCIL FOR PACIFIC AFFAIRS
NEW ZEALAND INSTITUTE OF INTERNATIONAL AFFAIRS
PAKISTAN INSTITUTE OF INTERNATIONAL AFFAIRS
PHILIPPINE COUNCIL, INSTITUTE OF PACIFIC RELATIONS
ROYAL INSTITUTE OF INTERNATIONAL AFFAIRS

INTERNATIONAL SECRETARIAT
1 EAST 54TH STREET, NEW YORK 22, N.Y.

REPRESENTATIVE GOVERNMENT IN SOUTHEAST ASIA

BY

RUPERT EMERSON

Professor of Government, Harvard University
Author of *Malaysia*

With Supplementary Chapters by
WILLARD H. ELSBREE *and*
VIRGINIA THOMPSON

*Issued under the auspices of the
Institute of Pacific Relations*

HARVARD UNIVERSITY PRESS
Cambridge, Massachusetts, 1955

All Rights Reserved
Copyright, 1955, by the
International Secretariat
INSTITUTE OF PACIFIC RELATIONS
1 East 54th St., New York 22, N.Y.

PRINTED IN THE UNITED STATES OF AMERICA

Foreword

ONE OF THE most baffling problems confronting the political leaders of the new nations of Southeast Asia, especially those with a long history of subjection to colonial rule, is how to develop, hastily and in an alien soil, those institutions and traditions of representative government which took so many decades to grow in Europe and America. Though most of these leaders, and many of the intellectual and administrative elite in the new countries, are committed by the constitutions of their countries and also by personal conviction to the principles of political democracy, and in most cases to the parliamentary form of government, they have to apply these principles in societies long accustomed to traditions of benevolent autocracy, quasi-feudal rule, or Western colonialism and lacking those driving forces of individualism, religious dissent, intellectual freedom and private business enterprise which played such crucial roles in the growth of representative government in the West. Yet the great experiment, some would say the great gamble, has already begun and is not likely to be reversed or stopped. The leaders and the peoples alike are caught in a swelling flood which they can only to a very limited extent control or canalize by still frail political institutions and administrative machinery.

The resultant dangers to both internal and international political stability in this danger spot of Asia are obvious enough. The desperate eleventh-hour struggle to create a viable non-Communist state in southern Vietnam is only the most striking and discouraging example. The dangers would be serious enough in times of international tranquillity and economic prosperity. They are doubly acute at a time when the pressure of Chinese Communism and the tensions of the Cold War are combined with economic instability aggravated by the slump in the prices of rice and the raw material exports of this region.

The present volume arises from a research project begun several years ago under the auspices of the Institute of Pacific Relations, partly as an adjunct to its studies of nationalism and Communism in Southeast Asia. It is intended to supplement an earlier brief study, *Parliamentary Government in Southern Asia,* by Mr. Sydney D. Bailey of the Hansard Society, London (dealing with India, Pakistan, Ceylon and Burma). Neither of the volumes is to be regarded as a definitive treatment of what is inevitably a rapidly expanding subject, but it is hoped that they will serve to arouse interest on the part of both Asian and Western scholars and political leaders and pave the way for more intensive inquiries at close range.

Limitations of time, opportunities for field investigation, and documentary sources have made it necessary to devote only slight attention to two important areas—Indochina and Thailand (both of which are discussed briefly in the final chapter). For different reasons the development of effective representative government in both countries has been retarded and it still remains to be seen how far it can flourish amid the pressures of Vietminh Communism on one side and military oligarchy on the other. Some glimpses of the problem in these two countries may be had, however, in three other IPR studies, *The Struggle for Indochina* by Ellen J. Hammer, *The Viet Minh Regime* by Bernard B. Fall, and *Some Aspects of Siamese Politics* by John Coast. Certain other aspects are treated in earlier studies, *Public Administration in Malaya* by S. W. Jones, *Public Administration in Burma* by F. S. V. Donnison, and *Public Administration in Siam* by W. D. Reeve (all issued under the joint auspices of the Royal Institute of International Affairs and the IPR).

The Institute officers are particularly indebted to Professor Rupert Emerson for undertaking the main part of the study and arranging the collaboration of Professor Elsbree, and also to Mrs. Virginia Thompson Adloff for her chapter on local government.

New York, January 1955

WILLIAM L. HOLLAND
Secretary General

Contents

	Foreword by W. L. Holland	v
I.	INTRODUCTION	3
II.	INDONESIA	17
III.	BURMA	41
IV.	MALAYA	58
V.	THE PHILIPPINES *by Willard H. Elsbree*	92
VI.	RURAL AND URBAN SELF-GOVERNMENT IN SOUTHEAST ASIA *by Virginia Thompson*	118
VII.	CONCLUSION	151
	THAILAND	159
	INDOCHINA	170
	Index	193

REPRESENTATIVE GOVERNMENT
IN SOUTHEAST ASIA

"*We have recognized in representative government the ideal type of the most perfect polity, for which, in consequence, any portion of mankind are better adapted in proportion to their degree of general improvement.* . . . *First, then, representative government, like any other government, must be unsuitable in any case in which it cannot permanently subsist—i.e., in which it does not fulfill the three fundamental conditions.* . . . *(1) That the people should be willing to receive it. (2) That they should be willing and able to do what is necessary for its preservation. (3) That they should be willing and able to fulfill the duties and discharge the functions which it imposes on them.*"

John Stuart Mill
Representative Government, Ch. IV

CHAPTER ONE

Introduction

THE PEOPLES of Southeast Asia have been thrust—or have thrust themselves—into an active role on the world stage at a time of peculiar difficulty and challenge. A brief listing of the major elements of world and local catastrophe which have impinged upon them can easily be read as pronouncing virtually a death sentence upon their efforts to establish and maintain effective, independent, and democratic governments. Emerging slowly from long periods of colonial rule, they were first caught in the toils of a world depression. As they struggled up toward economic recovery they were overwhelmed by the Japanese attack which, almost in a matter of days, shattered the established imperial bonds. To the devastation and destruction of war and the years of oppressive Japanese occupation there was added a liberation which in most instances brought with it further disorder, civil war, and rebellion; and the postwar world in which they sought or achieved independence was not one of peace but of cold war, torn by the gigantic conflict of the Communist and non-Communist blocs.

Such things as these obviously do not provide the setting in which the relatively fragile and intricate instrumentalities of representative institutions might best be expected to evolve and mature. Yet it is arguable that without them not only would the political status of the Southeast Asian countries be far less advanced but even that for some purposes they have made a positive contribution to domestic political advancement. Although it appears to be clearly written on the historical record that free institutions flourish most successfully where the external and internal stresses and strains are least urgent, in the special circumstances of Southeast Asia catastrophe served as a sharp sword to cut the new order loose from the old.

The most basic proposition of all must surely be that the series of crises through which the peoples of Southeast Asia have passed shattered old established institutions, relationships, and ways of action. The cake of custom was broken, and both the forces seeking dynamic change and the opportunities for securing change were multiplied. The goals which relatively limited circles of nationalists had set for their societies now came within reach, and the revolutionary ferment reached deep down into the ranks of the formerly voiceless and passive masses—far deeper, generally, than was in any way expected by the returning colonial authorities. Whether it had all moved too speedily and before the ground was properly prepared is an "if" to which there can be no more than a purely speculative answer, but it is beyond doubt that there was a great speeding up of any timetable of change which might plausibly have been foreseen.

More particularly, the world economic depression forced on both colonial governments and on the peoples themselves a re-appraisal of their position and a greater effort to develop their own resources and diversify their economic life. The war, the overthrow of the accustomed colonial rule, and the substitution of Japanese overlordship brought a new evaluation of relative strengths and abilities, a heightened sense of national unity, in many instances a greater opportunity for the peoples to manage their own affairs, and in the later stages a deliberate Japanese effort to encourage independence movements. In Indonesia and

Indochina, the brief interval between the Japanese surrender and the arrival of the Allied forces gave an opportunity to establish national governments and to organize or consolidate resistance and other armed forces on a more or less national basis.

The end of the war inaugurated a new era in the affairs of Southeast Asia, opening the door of self-government to peoples formerly held under colonial rule. In the case of Thailand there was a restoration of full sovereign independence, and for the Philippines an immediate resumption of the planned progress toward independence which had been initiated a decade earlier. After a period of serious difficulty but without open warfare, Burma achieved its separate sovereign existence at the beginning of 1948, breaking its ties with the Commonwealth, and nearly two years later Indonesia, after much sporadic fighting and two major military conflicts, transformed its subordination to the Netherlands into an equal association within a somewhat nominal union. The checkered history of Indochina in the postwar years lends itself to no easy summary, but the independence of the three countries which compose it, within or outside of the French Union, appears a foregone conclusion and has already secured at least formal recognition. Only in Malaya, disrupted by guerrilla warfare and deep-running racial divisions, has the colonial status carried over to the present day, still only meagerly tempered by an approach to self-governing institutions.

It is a striking fact that all the countries of Southeast Asia which have had an opportunity to shape their destinies freely have adopted constitutions which are basically modeled on well-established Western patterns, rather than seeking inspiration from their own remoter past or that of other Asian peoples. Under the guidance of the largely Westernized elites which have been the spearheads of the nationalist movements everywhere, the constitution makers have turned to Western Europe and the United

States to furnish the experience on which they might draw. It is notorious that in making the brief but stormy passage across the English Channel from Britain to France the parliamentary system underwent a drastic change. In Southeast Asia the effort of the peoples to adapt to their own use the Western institutions of representative government is being made across far greater distances of time, of culture, and of race; and it is only reasonable to expect that their Western-style representative institutions will in due course develop particular attributes of their own which will differentiate them sharply from their prototypes. The short life-span of these experiments and the extraordinary circumstances, both internal and external, under which they are being conducted make it obviously impossible to hope now to come to anything approaching definite conclusions as to their future fate; but, however tentative and hesitant the results which it may be possible to achieve, most careful and searching analysis deserves to be devoted to their experience.

On all scores the attempt to undertake such an analysis now is an exceedingly hazardous one. To put the hazards in the largest terms: on one side we do not have anything approaching adequate theoretical tools and certainties, establishing, as a distillation from the historical record, the conditions under which representative institutions can effectively flourish; on the other side, we do not have anything approaching adequate information of a detailed and intimate character about the actual course which the governments and peoples of Southeast Asia have taken in running their own affairs. Furthermore, there is no necessary *a priori* reason to assume that any generalizations of significance can be arrived at even for the six major areas of the region, leaving aside the lesser political divisions such as North Borneo and Portuguese Timor. Although there are certain common strands which run through all of them, the several countries differ in such fundamentals as ethnic composition, cultural and religious background, geopolitical position, and historical experience. Unless we knew with substantially greater assurance than we in fact do which are the determining elements in the successful functioning of the democratic process, it would obviously be impossible to come to confident conclusions as to the identity or diversity of the destiny of the different peoples.

Even though their weighting and significance for the development of representative institutions must be uncertain, there are several important elements common to Southeast Asia which must be of some measure of relevance.

Politically, all save Thailand (which by no means wholly escaped the impact of imperialism although it retained its political independence) have been in a colonial status for periods ranging from several decades to several centuries. The consequences of this status are too numerous, complex, and subtle to be elaborated in any brief compass, but a few may be suggested. The effective working experience of the peoples, at least at the central and intermediate levels, has been with a Western type of political institution, but at the bottom the village communities, embracing the mass of the agricultural population, have often remained relatively undisturbed. Colonialism has also inevitably meant everywhere, with the partial exception of the Philippines during the Commonwealth period from 1935 to 1946, that the positions in the top brackets of the government, the positions involving the power and responsibility of ultimate decision, were in the hands of the alien rulers and that a far from adequate number of native inhabitants of the countries were either trained for or experienced in the running of their own governments. Confronted by the manifold tasks of managing their entire political systems for international as well as domestic purposes, not to mention such additional problems as the building up of armed forces, developing and diversifying their economic life, and expanding their educational facilities, the new national states have found themselves dismayingly short both of experts and of political leaders.

Furthermore, it is a matter of very real consequence that frequently the most vigorous kind of political life and activity has been that of the nationalist or Communist opposition, attacking the existing colonial government root and branch. This tradition of opposition to government found further opportunity to blossom in the period of Japanese occupation and in some instances in the struggle to achieve liberation from the postwar colonial liberators. Nowhere, again with the partial exception of the Philippines, has there been any full experience of the practices and principles of democracy in any of its varied senses either in the older traditions of the peoples or in the colonial era. The individualism and egalitarianism which have been an essential part of the underpinning of democracy in the West have not generally been present in the Asian tradition; there has not been a sense of broad popular participation in a government felt to be an emanation from and responsive to the popular will; and governments have not been based upon the election of representatives endowed with responsibility for the management of the society.

Economically Southeast Asia is characterized for the most part by the poverty of the vast mass of its inhabitants and by the production of foodstuffs and raw materials, either for home consumption or for export. The existence of a dual economy made up of two sharply contrasting sectors has been typical: production for home consumption, notably of foodstuffs, has generally been carried on by the small-scale native producer, utilizing the traditional techniques of the society, whereas much of the production for export has been organized on a large-scale basis by foreign capital and enterprise. In the latter sphere the technical and managerial skills have usually been contributed by aliens while the local population has contributed the labor

INTRODUCTION

force and the secretarial and lower white-collar group. Capitalism, in part through the inescapable facts of the case and in part through the wide spread of Lenin's theory of imperialism, has been associated by the leaders and in the popular mind with the alien imperial regimes. Insofar as free enterprise is a necessary ingredient in the maintenance of a liberal and democratic system—a point on which there is by no means full agreement—the prospects for liberalism in Southeast Asia are relatively dim, particularly in view of the probability that the future will see more rather than less government intervention in the economy.

At least for present purposes the same conclusion must be reached in relation to that somewhat amorphous entity, the middle class, which has frequently been regarded as a central factor in the growth and stability of representative institutions. Throughout Southeast Asia it has been the general rule that both commerce and large-scale production have been carried on by aliens, either European or Chinese, and the indigenous middle class is slight in numbers and has no stake in the economic life of the several countries comparable to that of its counterparts in the West. There is, however, every reason to assume that as the new national governments increasingly take hold of the situation and move ahead with economic development the native bourgeoisie will rapidly multiply, even though their status may approximate more closely that of civil servants than of free entrepreneurs. But it must be recognized that despite much talk and planning and a considerable flurry of activity in the last few years under the impetus of the newly fashionable drive for the development of underdeveloped areas, there has still been relatively little in the way of economic diversification and of industrialization.

This situation is beginning slowly to change as domestic and international development projects come into operation, but it seems all too clear that the movement toward a modernization of economic systems and a significant raising of the standards of living will be a long and difficult one. In the interval, the native middle class will continue to be a thin layer of men representing rather the professions and government service than the independent or quasi-independent business group which has been its mainstay in the West in the past.

In the elusive cultural realm it is even more difficult than it is in others to single out those elements which are of special relevance for the effective survival of representative institutions. Perhaps the most important as well as the most obvious thing which can be said is that the basic cultural heritage of the peoples of Southeast Asia is totally different from that of the peoples of Western Europe who were the creators of representative government and have continued as its most successful practitioners, either at home or in the new countries to which they have migrated. There is neither need nor occasion to leap to any racialist argument which at some not unprecedented extreme, might equate political ability or a unique flair for democracy with white skins; but it is certainly plausible to assume that a people's heritage of ways of life and thought must have a significant bearing both on the original shaping of political institutions and on the way in which they evolve. To those who would derive the political institutions of the West primarily from the heritage of Greece and Rome and of Christianity it is self-evident that an effort on the part of Asians to adopt such institutions for their own use could at the best have very limited success. At all events, what would in due course emerge would have only an accidental resemblance to the model from which it was drawn.

The situation is made markedly more complex by one centrally important factor which has already been mentioned. The persons who in fact have guided the rising destinies of the Southeast Asian nations are, with only the rarest exceptions, the new and highly Westernized elites whose political thinking and experience have been shaped in the main in the Western mold. In the drafting of constitutions, although they have taken bits and pieces eclectically from other systems, they have tended to be sharply influenced by the political structure of the imperial center from which they are separating. A striking illustration of this trend is the adoption by the Philippines of the American presidential-system, based on the separation of powers, as contrasted with the general adoption of the parliamentary form elsewhere. Although the analogy is in many respects unfair and should certainly not be pressed too far, it may be suggested that just as the colonial governments were imposed on the people from above and outside, so the new Western-style constitutions have been the work of small groups whose intellectual and, in a sense, political links are with the West rather than with the mass of their own people. In one degree or another these latter constitutions have been accorded a kind of national acceptance, formal or informal, which was in no way involved for the colonial regimes; but it remains the fact that they are substantially unrelated to the political traditions of the Southeast Asian countries. The bulk of the people have had no experience in the management of political systems of this variety. That strains and tensions, perhaps of a very grave order, are inherent in such a combination of the new and the old is too obvious to require any elaboration,[1] but

[1] J. S. Furnivall has delivered a frontal attack on the idea that progress can be secured through the adoption of full-scale democratic institutions. It is his contention that parliamentary government requires the existence of a social will for its effective operation and that where such a social will is lacking, as he finds it to be in the characteristically plural societies of Southeast Asia, parliamentary government is likely to disrupt rather than unite. Furthermore he contends that the necessity for these societies to make a speedy adaptation to the conditions of the modern world will run into inevitable difficulty where a parliament represents the tradition-bound mass of the population: "In the tropics people in general do not

to seek to specify the outcome with any particularity is a very different matter.

It must be admitted at the outset that there are here fundamental questions to which we do not know the answers with any measure of certainty. What are the basic or most significant preconditions for the successful survival of representative institutions? We know that in fact on the basis of the historical record to date they have evolved in a Western world which has its own peculiar ethical, religious, and cultural traditions, and that it has been a slow growth over many centuries. To what extent are they based on the fundamental elements of a way of life, on a *Weltanschauung*, which is not shared, and may in fact even be repudiated by peoples whose traditional attachment is to societies and philosophies which head in quite different directions? Or, approaching the problem from a different angle, to what extent do they derive from the unique and peculiar type of economic system which, itself obviously related in some fashion to the cultural background, has played so large a role in revolutionizing the societies of the West? It may be that the answers are to be found in these subtle and complex realms, but the questions raised are of so profound and delicate a character as to leave them almost necessarily in the realm of philosophical speculation. If one or more of the Southeast Asian countries succeeds in making representative institutions work, it is legitimate to conclude that the cultural and economic differences are not matters of the first importance; but if they were to fail, it would still be possible to place the blame on a number of other factors, internal and external, which could legitimately be regarded as making success impossible.

To proceed with scientific exactitude there should ap-

---

want what the conditions of the modern world necessitate, and self-government consequently does not give them what they want" (p. 455). *Colonial Policy and Practice*, Cambridge, 1948, Chapters XI and XII.

pear at this stage, if not substantially earlier, a precise definition of what is meant by representative institutions. The temptation is, however, strong, and perhaps desirably irresistible, to evade precise definition and to assume that the general confines of what is meant by representative institutions are commonly understood and that no effort to pin them down in rigorous detail could embrace the multiplicity of acceptable variants.

In a recent report on a closely related theme, the Hansard Society has described what may be regarded as some of the characteristics and aims of parliamentary government in terms which seem equally applicable to the somewhat broader category of representative government.[2] At the head of their list appears the proposition that "the executive government should be answerable to and dismissible by the people or their chosen representatives, and should be subject to the law as interpreted by the judiciary." This is followed by a series of further propositions such as that laws should be enacted by a popularly elected legislature; that the judiciary should be independent; that citizens should be free to hold and express opinions, and to organize political parties which can offer themselves as an alternative government; that elections should be free and impartially conducted; and that access to the public service should be open to all on the basis of merit.

These admirable formulations might be supplemented by the addition of another point of a more general nature. In order to function effectively representative institutions require more than anything else a deep and working sense of democracy based on a feeling of some real measure of equality of the different individuals, groups, and classes composing the society. Furthermore there must be a widespread sense that government is an instrument of the people which they can utilize to achieve their own purposes

[2] Hansard Society, *Problems of Parliamentary Government in Colonies*, London, 1953, pp. 2–4.

and to benefit their own lives and with which they identify themselves at least to some degree. The assumption that government is something remote, superior, and perhaps even alien must be replaced by the assumption that the ordinary man has a stake in it and that he is given an opportunity to participate actively in its operations at one or another level. Both in fact and in the popular consciousness, government must be subject to the ultimate control of the people and responsive to their interests. Where a sense of identification with the government is lacking, particularly in countries where political experience is slight and illiteracy is the rule rather than the exception, the constitutional forms and trappings of democracy may well serve only as a meager cloak for rule by the few who have been able to draw power into their own hands.

One danger involved in setting up criteria such as these for the successful functioning of representative institutions is that they may be taken as counsels of perfection and as setting standards for the newcomers to the ranks of independent states higher than those achieved by their older-established brethren who have been operating representative systems for several generations with greater or less skill. Certainly a watchful eye must be kept on those critics, perhaps particularly likely to turn up among the old colonial hands, who would take an ill-disguised pleasure in the failures and misfortunes of the former colonial wards. If, on one hand, it is obvious that the all too evident sins and shortcomings of the Western democracies should not be taken as a model by Asian peoples or as an excuse for their own shortcomings, it would, on the other hand, be absurd to expect a record of spotless performance from the most recent recruits to the democratic art.

The circumstances under which the new Southeast Asian states are compelled to launch their constitutional ventures lend special urgency to such a warning. Apart from such more general issues as the cultural background and political tradition, the almost universal poverty and mass illiteracy, the years immediately preceding independence have worked to produce situations which render the flourishing of representative institutions, painful enough to manage in the most favorable setting, almost intolerably difficult.

Furthermore the Southeast Asian countries are coming to independent self-government not only at the close of the period of social disruption inherent in colonialism, but after the shattering experience of war and revolution. Leaving independent Thailand aside, only in the Philippines has there been a reasonably smooth and agreed transition to freedom from the colonial yoke. The period of Japanese occupation fostered many developments and forces which have been useful for the newly independent countries, but it also put arms in the hands of many of the young men and accustomed them to their use. For many the habits of regular and productive labor were lost, and conspiratorial resistance and freebooting became a way of life. Inevitably the achievement of independence had been pictured as the start of a golden age; when independence as an accomplished fact brought virtually none of the answers and meant not only no lifting of the burdens but even an increase of them, the temptation to resort to violence was very great for those considerable elements in the society which had lost a sense of discipline and social cohesion. In the background, or in the forefront, everywhere were the Communists, seeking to encourage disruption and upheaval and holding out as in their possession the golden age which the nationalists were demonstrably unable to produce. It would be asking for the moon to expect that in such circumstances representative institutions could be set in motion without an accompaniment of turmoil, of corruption, of deep-running social cleavage, and of trends toward both disintegration and authoritarianism. If it is plausible to suggest that a democratic system of government must be based upon a relatively homogeneous society and requires a period of peace and internal stability to get itself established, then Southeast Asia obviously falls short of these prerequisites.

The question may indeed be asked as to the propriety of establishing the ability effectively to manage representative institutions as one of the major criteria in judging the political record and prospects of Southeast Asian countries. To find an adequate answer it is not necessary to undertake an elaborate inquiry into the validity of the prevailing belief in the universal value and virtue of democracy, nor to deny that other forms of government have proved themselves viable and successful. Leaving these larger and more debatable issues aside, it would seem appropriate to rest the case on the proposition that with unbroken uniformity the political leaders of Southeast Asia, backed by the apparent support of their peoples, have themselves chosen the path of constitutional representative government. Clearly no problem of the imposition of alien standards need be involved where the goals are those which the Southeast Asians have freely set for themselves.

CHAPTER TWO

Indonesia

As by far the largest and most populous of the countries of Southeast Asia, the Republic of Indonesia is necessarily a focal point of interest. Its population of seventy-five to eighty million is perhaps three times that of its nearest rival, Indochina, and its strategic position and its impressive economic resources and potentialities establish it as one of the key middle powers for the purposes of world politics. Through the adherence of the overwhelming majority of its people to Islam it achieves significant bonds to the rest of the Moslem world, and in the postwar years it has built up particularly close ties with India, to whose nationalist movement the Indonesian leaders had often turned for inspiration during the interwar decades. Its prompt acceptance into the United Nations following the formal transfer of sovereignty by the Netherlands on December 27, 1949, placed the final seal of international recognition on its independent existence. Since that time it has played a significant role in international affairs as a leading member of the "third force" Asian-Arab bloc.

The problems confronting Indonesia in its new-found independence are complex and formidable, but it has been a staunch adherent to the democratic creed since its first declaration of independence in the wild days of the close of the war with Japan. Unlike the Philippines which, despite the period of Japanese occupation, moved toward sovereign statehood along an agreed path with fixed milestones, Indonesia came to independence the hard way. Whatever the actual intentions of the Dutch may have been in regard to ultimate freedom for Indonesia, they in fact twice launched what were euphemistically termed police actions which forced the Indonesians to devote much of their energy and limited resources to military preparation and to open armed conflict. If the progress of Indonesia toward stable and efficient self-government has been somewhat halting and uncertain, this must in large measure be attributed to the roadblocks which were placed in its way.

On all scores the training for self-government which the Indonesians received from the Dutch in the centuries of colonial rule fell far short of what was necessary and desirable. There is no occasion to attempt to review here the long and intricate history of Dutch management of the Indies but, after one has exhausted the substantial catalog of the virtues of Dutch rule, it is impossible to avoid the conclusion that not only were many things left undone which might have been done but also that, at the rate of prior progress, a full Indonesian readiness for independence could not have been expected until some remote time in the future. In order to measure the gap between accomplishment and need it is by no means necessary to leap to the conclusion that the Dutch regime was one of sinful exploitation or that the Dutch more than other colonial powers thwarted the legitimate advancement of their wards. By the turn of the century the blacker days of the Company and of the Culture System were well past, and new and more enlightened policies were being followed; but, to put it in the mildest terms, there was very little in the way of an eager and vigorous Dutch effort to set the Indonesians firmly on the road toward independence.

Economically, although the Indies were built up into the position of being one of the world's key suppliers of raw materials, there was relatively little in the way of industrialization, even after the depression had demonstrated the striking vulnerability of the economy. Furthermore, the management and the profits of economic life above the level of the small native producer of rice, rubber or other agricultural goods tended to be in European or in Chinese hands, and the per capita income of the Indonesians was among the lowest for the world's peoples. On the other side of the ledger, it was one of the abiding merits of the Dutch system that, in contrast to the Philippines, no significant class of large landlords was created or allowed to come into existence, thus eliminating one of the major problems which has plagued other countries. In sum, although the basic wealth of Indonesia is great, its people are poverty-stricken, it is tragically weak in technical and managerial manpower, its modern-style economic enterprises are very largely in alien control, and it has exceedingly little in the way of capital on which it can draw for the development of its potentialities.

Culturally the Indonesians, like other Southeast Asian peoples, were in slow process of transition from their own highly developed and traditional culture to some still unforeseeable adaptation to the forces and ideas of the contemporary world. The past policy of the Dutch had on the whole been one of maintaining the existing native society and of not encouraging the Westernization of Indonesians, but under a number of pressures this policy had at least been relaxed during the present century. By the end of the period of Dutch rule there had appeared a substantial corps of new leaders equipped with either a full acquaintance with the modes of thought and action of the West or a reasonable approximation thereof; but this group constituted only a tiny fragment of the entire population. For the latter, education in any formal sense remained the exception rather than the rule: at the time of the Japanese occupation under 10 percent of the people had achieved literacy. An indication of the very limited scope of education at higher levels is given by the frequently cited fact that in 1940 only 240 Indonesian students were graduated from the high schools of the archipelago and only 37 from the colleges. The expanding Dutch educational system had obviously hardly even made a beginning in meeting the needs of a population of seventy million or more. If there were in the new elite which was rising to the top a few who had a wide and effective consciousness of the world at large, the great mass of the people was still tied close, both physically and spiritually, to the village and the market town.

In the political sphere the interwar decades witnessed a growing participation by Indonesians but the ultimate control remained firmly embraced in the Dutch grasp. On the administrative side George McT. Kahin reports that "as late as October 1940, out of the 3,039 higher-rank civil service positions only 221 were held by Indonesians";[1] and even in the middle civil service ranks there continued to be large numbers of Europeans, including Eurasians who, under the Dutch system, were counted for all formal and legal purposes as Europeans. A series of representative bodies, culminating at the national level in the Volksraad, gave some opportunity for the formation and expression of public opinion, but their powers were carefully limited and checked. Based on a small electorate which operated through an indirect electoral process, the Volksraad was given an increasing share in legislation and unquestionably exercised a significant influence but its powers were generally not final or decisive. Furthermore, even in its fullest

[1] *Nationalism and Revolution in Indonesia*, Ithaca, 1952, p. 34. The remainder of this chapter owes so heavy a debt to this basic work by Mr. Kahin and to his section on "Indonesian Politics and Nationalism" in *Asian Nationalism and the West*, edited by William L. Holland (New York, 1953), that it has been thought better to make a general and grateful acknowledgment at this point than to attempt to footnote each particular item.

bloom it contained only 30 Indonesians as against 25 Europeans, 5 non-Indonesian Asiatics, and a chairman appointed by the Crown. Of this membership 20 Indonesians, 15 Europeans, and 3 other Asiatics were elected, the remainder being appointed by the Governor-General.

The importance of the Volksraad as a channel for the expression of Indonesian political views was further limited by the fact that many of the nationalist leaders declined to participate in it. Nor was it without basic relevance that, particularly during the 1930's, a number of the outstanding nationalists were spending a great deal of their time in Dutch jails or concentration camps, not appearing again on the political scene until the arrival of the Japanese. Through the public service and the regency and through the provincial councils and the Volksraad a relatively large number of Indonesians came to have some acquaintance with modern political processes and representative institutions, but neither the quantity of those involved nor the limited powers and responsibilities entrusted to them were in any sense adequate to the tasks which independence thrust upon them.

The brief declaration of independence issued by Sukarno on August 17, 1945, was the signal for a swift series of actions which succeeded in endowing Indonesia with an operating government in the vitally important weeks that intervened before the first landing of the British. The central agency for this purpose was the Indonesian Independence Preparatory Committee which had been set up shortly before with Japanese consent and consisted of twenty-one nationalists drawn from all parts of the archipelago. One of the first actions of this body was the promulgation of a somewhat hastily drafted constitution for the Republic of Indonesia, and the naming as president and vice-president of Sukarno and Hatta, who have continued in these offices to the present day through all the changes of political fortune and structure. At the end of

August the first cabinet of the new republic was formed, made up of a combination of newcomers and of men who had served under the Japanese.

Of the constitution there is no need to speak in detail, not only because it was sketchy and clearly provisional in character but also because it was never brought into very effective operation. Of more importance than its details were the general principles which lay behind it and which derive from the *Pantjasila* (the Five Principles)—the fundamentals of the political philosophy of the new Indonesia —which had been laid out by Sukarno in a speech of June 1, 1945. These Five Principles, which have been regularly reiterated and redefined by Sukarno and others and appear again in the preamble to the present constitution, are: recognition of divine omnipotence, with freedom for each person to believe in his own God; nationalism, which must embrace the whole territory of the Indies; internationalism or humanism, which can only be based upon a firmly established nationalism; democracy, which involves representative government, popular sovereignty, and the principle of consent; and social justice, which rounds out democracy in the economic sphere.

One institutional feature which deserves special comment because of the controversies which later developed around it was the centrality of the position given to the president. Although the president was to be elected by the People's Congress (which in fact never came into existence), his powers approximated or even exceeded those of the president of the United States, and a presidential, as opposed to a parliamentary, system was explicitly envisaged. Thus it was provided that the president should be commander-in-chief of the armed forces and control the conduct of foreign affairs; that he should have a strong share in the legislative power and in time of emergency enact ordinances with the force of law; that he should be vested with the executive power; and that the members of his cabinet should be appointed and discharged at his pleasure. In the actual evolution of constitutional principle and practice, the parliamentary system came to acceptance at an early day, but the role of the president has developed in a markedly distinctive fashion, in large part no doubt because of the personality, strength, and popular hold of Sukarno.

Since no general election has ever been held, the foundations on which the representative institutions of the republic rest have always necessarily been somewhat shaky. In its transitional provisions the first constitution stated that the Preparatory Committee should bridge the immediate gap and that until the new representative bodies were elected their powers should be exercised by the president assisted by a national committee. This body—the Central Indonesian National Committee—was created at the end of August 1945, with a membership of 135 persons selected to include the principal nationalist leaders and to represent a wide array of the groupings and interests of the islands. By mid-November, with the agreement of Sukarno and Hatta, the National Committee had achieved a considerable political revolution which set a new constitutional course. Leaving aside the personalities and forces which brought them about, the innovations may be lumped under three closely interrelated headings. In the first place, the Committee succeeded in elevating itself from an essentially advisory status to that of a body with legislative powers, but, secondly, it vested the normal exercise of its power in a Working Committee which promptly became one of the central instrumentalities of government. Thirdly, it buttressed its new-found powers by a reversal of the previous decision to follow the American presidential pattern and secured the creation of a cabinet responsible to itself, headed by Sjahrir.

The presently operative provisional constitution of the

Republic of Indonesia, promulgated on August 15, 1950, continues the principle of parliamentary government, although the accompanying official elucidation issued by the Minister of Justice states that "in exigencies, however, the Cabinet may again become a Presidential one." Under this constitution the president, whose mode of election is to be specified by law, is designated as the head of the state and plays a significant part in the making of cabinets, as practice has amply demonstrated, through his power to appoint one or more cabinet formateurs, and, in accordance with their recommendation, to appoint the prime minister and the other ministers. In two successive counterbalancing articles it is provided that the ministers shall be jointly responsible for the entire policy of the government and each minister individually for his share in the government, and that the president has the right to dissolve the House of Representatives. The legislative power is vested in the government (i.e., the executive branch) and the House of Representatives acting in concurrence with each other, but the government is given the right to enact emergency laws subject to review by the House at its next meeting at the latest.

This deviation from the original intention to establish a presidential system might appear to have elevated the president to a lofty but inconsequential eminence, but the working pattern which has developed would not justify such a conclusion. To define the role which the president in the person of Sukarno has actually played is by no means an easy matter and would require a very intimate knowledge of much that has gone on behind the scenes in Indonesian politics. If he has not had either the formal or the substantive position of the president of the United States, it is equally clear that he has been a political force and personage of much greater consequence than the president of France, whose role is primarily symbolic and representational. Sukarno, who is both a statesman of the modern world and an orator with an unrivalled popular appeal to the masses, has declared that he is neither an American nor a French president but "a president of the Indonesian revolution." He has certainly not interpreted his function as being that of a symbolic figurehead, but he has also normally abstained from any effort to control the day to day business of government.

All available evidence indicates that Sukarno has remained from the beginning the most potent single individual in Indonesia, and perhaps the best formulation of the part which he has played would be to say that he has served throughout as the presiding political genius, keeping a watchful eye over the general development and trends of the Indonesian society and intervening forcefully, or at the least persuasively, in times of crisis. Since times of crisis have been the rule rather than the exception, he has frequently been in the forefront. Without seeking to delve into the behind-the-scenes activities of the president, which have been particularly significant in relation to the frequent demise and reconstruction of cabinets, two illustrations may be given of his assumption of power under emergency conditions. Both at the time of the kidnaping of Premier Sjahrir in June 1946 and at the time of the Madiun Communist rising in September 1948, absolute authority was vested in Sukarno; and in a different type of crisis when the Sjarifuddin government fell in January 1948, he promptly appointed a "presidential" cabinet headed by Hatta, but this cabinet appears not in fact to have regarded its relations to the parliamentary majority as different from those of other cabinets.

Another striking manifestation of the president's power was the decree which he issued in December 1946 increasing the membership of the National Committee from 200 to 514 and in some respects drastically changing its composition. When this action was challenged in the Working Committee, the issue was referred to the full National Committee which allowed the presidential decree to stand. Sukarno's own view of his position was clearly mirrored in his statement that until popular election of the representative bodies becomes possible, "it is the task of the President himself to nominate and appoint members because of the fact that the President himself is regarded as the representative of the whole people."[2] This and many other statements and actions can leave no doubt that in the unstable and revolutionary conditions existing in Indonesia it has been Sukarno's conviction that a strong hand must be maintained at the center and a reserve presidential power kept in existence to take over when grave dangers threatened.

Sukarno as president has been a key element of strength and continuity in the new Indonesia, but there has been a much larger degree of instability and flux in the successive central representative assemblies and the series of cabinets which have risen and fallen with almost monotonous regularity. As far as the latter are concerned, it is, however, not unreasonable to contend that the appearance of change has been somewhat larger than the reality. Although a number of new faces have made their appearance from time to time, not infrequently the overturn of one cabinet and the creation of another has, as in France, meant not very much more than a reshuffle of posts within substantially the same group of people, and, at least to the external observer, the differences in program and policy from one cabinet to another have been relatively slight and insignificant. It is difficult to evade the conclusion that what has often been involved is less a matter of divergences in goals and methods than the clash of personalities and ambitions.

[2] Cited by Kahin, *Nationalism and Revolution in Indonesia*, p. 202.

A recent commentator has pointed out the weakness of the present cabinet system in the following terms:[3]

"The Indonesian cabinets have all been short-lived. Whenever a seriously divisive issue has arisen and a cabinet has taken resolute action on it, it has almost invariably fallen. . . . The cabinets of Natsir, Sukiman, and Wilopo were indeed all but hamstrung. Opposition between the parties, and especially between the Masjumi and P.N.I., was one important cause. A second cause was factionalism between the parties, and again particularly these two. The sentiment of utopian radicalism, a legacy from colonial days when Indonesians were permanently 'against' almost everything and had little or no political responsibility, manifested itself in a continuing failure to understand the realities a cabinet had to face. These two factors made resolute government virtually impossible for any cabinet unless it was prepared to run a great risk of being overthrown."

The representative bodies, lacking the firm foundation of popular roots which only general elections could have given them, have been somewhat divorced from the people whom they were to represent and their members have not been confronted by the challenge of conducting electoral campaigns which would bring them in direct touch with their constituents. The proportionate representation given in these bodies to the different political parties and interests has necessarily been based in considerable measure on guesswork and may throughout or at certain times in fact have been a quite misleading reflection of the actual division and balance of public opinion.

The forthcoming national election, long prepared for and often postponed, of a constituent assembly and parlia-

[3] Herbert Feith, "Toward Elections in Indonesia," *Pacific Affairs*, Sept. 1954, pp. 247–48. This article gives a somewhat detailed account of the difficulties involved in moving toward a general election in Indonesia and of the pressures for an election.

ment on the basis of the new electoral law which was promulgated on April 7, 1953, will for the first time make possible a more accurate assessment of the true strength of the several parties. In virtually every respect this law throws the door wide open to the fullest democratic expression of the political sentiments and preferences of the Indonesians.[4] The franchise is extended to all legally registered Indonesian citizens of eighteen years of age and over, and also to those who have been married or divorced even though they may be under eighteen. The voting is to be by secret ballot in a direct election although there was some sentiment for an indirect system; and candidates may be put forward on an individual basis, by parties, or by other groups. A complex system of proportional representation is intended to ensure that the ultimate result will accurately reflect the diversity of Indonesian opinion. For electoral purposes the country has been divided into sixteen districts (one of which, it should be noted in passing, is the disputed area of West Irian), with the provision that each district secure representation proportionate to its population. For the Constituent Assembly one representative will be elected for each 150,000 Indonesian citizens; for the House of Representatives there is to be one for each 300,000. The management of the election in its different phases has been entrusted to a hierarchy of special committees in five tiers ranging from locally appointed village registration committees at the bottom to the central election committee appointed by the president at the top.

The present House of Representatives is a product of the movement toward a unitary state and is the direct successor of several representative assemblies which preceded

[4] See Boyd R. Compton, "The Indonesian Election Law," *Far Eastern Survey*, April and May 1954. For an account of two recent elections, one on a direct basis in Minahasa and the other on an indirect basis in Jogjakarta, see *Indonesian Affairs*, Oct.–Nov. 1951, pp. 14–22; April–May 1952, pp. 10–18.

it on the Indonesian political scene.[5] Its membership at the time of its formation in 1950 consisted of an amalgamation of the leading bodies of the United States of Indonesia and the old Republic: the House of Representatives and the Senate of the former, and the Working Committee and the High Advisory Council of the latter. In the present Indonesian political setting one of the major difficulties of operating a system of parliamentary government involving cabinet responsibility arises from the fact that there is not only a multiplicity of parties, many of them triflingly small, but also nothing approaching a majority for any one of the larger parties. Out of a total membership in the House of well over 200, the two leading parties which have tended to alternate in power or occasionally to join in coalition governments, the Masjumi (Moslem) and the Nationalist, have respectively only 39 and 37 seats. The next in size is the Greater Indonesian Party (Persatuan Indonesia Raya) with 18 seats, followed by the Socialists and the Communists with 15 seats each.[6] While it is true that several reasonably durable groupings of parties have developed and that some of the non-party members have formed party attachments, the political base of any cabinet in the House is necessarily weak. Unless the returns from the national election are such as to eliminate some of the smaller political groupings and concentrate power effectively in the hands of two or three major parties, Indonesia will be condemned to an indefinite continuation of unstable coalition multi-party governments. It is generally accepted that the splinter parties will suffer serious losses in the election, but only the final counting of ballots will determine whether the net result is to produce a government with a

[5] For a brief history and analysis of the Indonesian parliamentary system, see J. H. A. Logemann, "The Indonesian Parliament," *Parliamentary Affairs*, Autumn 1953, pp. 346–53.

[6] *Report on Indonesia*, New York: Indonesian Information Office, May 7, 1953.

clear mandate for action or to underscore the elements of uncertainty and division.

One of the essential functions of parties in any political system is to serve as a link between the general populace in all its branches and segments and the governing groups which actually wield power. In a country such as Indonesia where there is a big, and perhaps even a dangerous, gap between the small Westernized elite at the top and the largely illiterate mass of the people whose horizons still tend to be confined to the village or the market town,[7] the need is peculiarly great and pressing for parties which effectively reach down to the grass roots. That the parties presently in existence in Indonesia adequately perform this function is open to the gravest doubt, although it is to be hoped that the forthcoming general election will by itself enforce a greater measure of grass roots activity. In recent years the trend, however, appears not to have been in this direction but rather toward a concentration of power and activity in the relatively small groups concerned with the central management of at least the major political parties.[8] Although there have been flurries of activity looking toward a broadening of the popular base of the parties —perhaps most notably in the case of the Masjumi—the results have been meager and there is a widespread sense that party affairs have come to be manipulated to too great an extent by a limited group of insiders. In the interwar decades it was a characteristic of the Indonesian political parties that they tended to cluster around particular leaders and personalities, and their shifting alliances and disagreements, rather than around coherent programs or ide-

[7] See Paul M. Kattenburg, *A Central Javanese Village in 1950*, Ithaca, 1951.

[8] "Leaving aside imposing paper claims of party membership, Indonesian political life is a kind of poker game played by a few thousand people all of whom have known each other much too long and too well." Robert C. Bone, Jr., "The Future of Indonesian Political Parties," *Far Eastern Survey*, Feb. 1954, p. 17.

ologies; and the same tendency has held true in the postwar period. One recent Indonesian analyst has presented his conclusions in the following terms:[9]

"The divided and chaotic party system in Indonesia is at present one of the great weaknesses of the nation. One can even say that what is happening in Indonesia at present is a failure of leadership. At the moment when the country needs them most, the leaders are squabbling with one another. There is no longer that unity of purpose and spirit which fused them during the revolutionary years. Instead there is confusion, suspicion, and weakness, and even more dangerous, there is also corruption."

Since the autumn of 1952 Indonesian political parties and personalities have been engaged in a complex and confused process of re-orientation which has embittered many relationships and in its ramifications has touched almost every aspect of the political life of the country. The controversy which set this process in motion centered around the program of the Sultan of Jogjakarta, in his capacity as Minister of Defense, for the reform and modernization of the army, including the elimination or subordination of some of the former guerrilla and resistance elements. On October 17, 1952, a popular demonstration of the Sultan's supporters against the Parliament brought the issue dramatically to public attention and set loose a chain of events the end of which is still not in sight.

No brief summary could do justice to the tangled political free-for-all which followed this threatening outburst but some of the broad lines of influence which radiated

[9] Mochtar Lubis, "Party Confusion in Indonesia," *Far Eastern Survey*, Oct. 29, 1952. See also the comments by Kahin in *Asian Nationalism and the West*, pp. 184–88, on the gap between the peasantry and the elite, and on "the dangerous social irresponsibility shown by a number of Indonesian political leaders, and particularly in the behavior of certain political parties in Parliament." *Indonesian Affairs* (Oct.–Nov.–Dec. 1952) presents a review by Roeslan Abdulgani, Secretary-General of the Ministry of Information, of Indonesian parties and their parliamentary role.

out from it are becoming reasonably clear. Somewhat miraculously the Wilopo government, which was in power at the time, survived the crisis for a number of months, but the coalition on which it was based became increasingly unworkable as the two major partners within it, the Nationalists and the Masjumi, drew further and further apart. In the conflict over the Sultan and his army program the Nationalists embraced the opposition position, while the Masjumi tended to give its backing to the Sultan whose clearest supporters were Sjahrir and the Socialist Party which he headed. It also became clear at an early stage that among the enemies of the Sultan was to be counted President Sukarno, whose leaning toward the Nationalists was demonstrated with growing openness. The Communist Party took pleasure in the mounting disagreements of their more bourgeois colleagues—and frequently lined up with the Nationalists.

Early in June 1953 the Wilopo government fell and an unprecedented stretch of fifty-eight days intervened before a new cabinet was formed. In the negotiations during this period Sukarno played a central role, and it is generally assumed that he had a major share of the responsibility for the coming to power on July 30 of the new coalition, now excluding the Masjumi, which had Ali Sastroamidjojo, former Ambassador to the United States, as its head and Dr. Wongsonegoro of the Greater Indonesian Party as Vice-Premier. Indeed, one commentator has suggested that, although this cabinet is technically constituted on a parliamentary basis, it "actually is 'presidential' in everything but name," since its Nationalist leaders are old and trusted compatriots of the President and "among the other members of the Cabinet there is not a single individual of sufficient prestige or independence to dare ignore the President's bidding."[10] A highly significant feature of the

[10] Robert C. Bone, Jr., *op. cit.*, p. 19.

working of the new government has been the development of disturbingly close ties between the Communists and the Nationalists, who have perhaps felt that they were losing ground in the country at large and who certainly needed support to maintain their slim and unsteady coalition in Parliament.

One of the most dangerous aspects of the clash between the Sultan, who resigned from his post as Defense Minister in January 1953, and his opponents was the serious threat that the army might be drawn into politics and used for political purposes. In the present conditions of Indonesia the possibilities of trouble in any incursion of the army into politics are too obvious to require elaboration. In a different guise a somewhat similar threat had been posed in the latter half of 1947 and early 1948 when the Ministry of Defense was headed by Amir Sjarifuddin, who built up a personal following in the army and has been charged with using his position for the spread of the Communist creed which he later openly avowed for himself at the time of the Madiun Communist uprising in September 1948. This threat was blocked by the presidential cabinet of Hatta which took office in January 1948, and succeeded in restoring the army to its proper role. In 1953 much the same problem arose when the Defense Minister in the Ali Sastroamidjojo cabinet proposed that arms should be given to a Communist-controlled group for the purpose of fighting Darul Islam. It should also be noted that in the aftermath of the controversy over the Sultan's proposals for army reform subordinate officers in several military posts, asserting their allegiance to President Sukarno, rose to overthrow regional commanders who adhered to the Minister of Defense. The control of the army and the question of its reorganization have continued as major issues confronting the government which took over in July 1953.

With the possible exception of the ever-present Communist issue, the most important development of the last year or two, which is clearly linked in a number of ways to the events which have just been discussed, is the increasing and open cleavage in relation to the role of Islam in the new Indonesian state and society. In its simplest form this may be stated in the question as to whether Indonesia is to become explicitly an Islamic state—although the implications of a decision to declare it constitutionally an Islamic state are far from clear and might in fact give rise to serious splits within the ranks of the Moslems themselves. The turn in the direction of more open consideration of this problem derived in part from the fellow-travelling of the Nationalists and the Communists, now in command of the government, which had its influence in urging the Masjumi toward a more forthright assertion of its Islamic base.[11] Another potent factor was the declaration of Sukarno early in 1953 that he favored a secular national state and feared the disruptive effect on the non-Moslem elements of the country of an Indonesian state based solely on Islam.

For the Masjumi, although it is avowedly an Islamic party, the raising of the religious issue was not without its embarrassments. A mass party, which is widely believed to have the largest popular hold in the country, it embraces not only the more traditionally-minded countryside but also the modernistically inclined urban and younger elements who inevitably play a significant role in the determination of its policies. Furthermore, there is the always troublesome issue of the relation between the Masjumi and the fanatically Moslem Darul Islam, which has maintained its hold for some years over considerable parts of West and Central Java. The Masjumi leaders cannot give open support to a movement which explicitly challenges the national government and yet there are evidences

[11] *The New York Times*, March 1, 1954, reported a mass protest meeting in Jakarta of 200,000 Moslems, organized in part by the Masjumi, against recent Nationalist and Communist insults to Islam.

of sympathy and direct links between the two which make drastic action against Darul Islam unpalatable to by no means negligible segments of the Masjumi Party. Inevitably the Nationalists and the Communists have not neglected the opportunity to exploit the discomfiture of their major rival on this score. The more recent rising in Acheh (in Sumatra), always a center of intense Islamic orthodoxy, has only served to complicate the issue further. There can be no doubt that one of the major questions with which the Constituent Assembly will have to deal will be the decision as to whether or not Indonesia is to be endowed with an explicit religious affiliation.

Another problem which remains to be brought to proper resolution, and which has been given greater urgency by the turmoil in the region of Acheh, is the nature, role, and structure of the lower governmental and administrative units in the future Indonesian political system.[12] The federal experiment of the Republic of the United States of Indonesia, which had a brief life of only a few months following the achievement of independence, was effectively doomed to failure before it started. It may be said that the Dutch delivered the kiss of death to it before its birth because the states of which it was composed were so largely Dutch creations, viewed with profound hostility and suspicion by the nationalists. The speedy transition to a unitary state was regarded as part of the necessary process of eliminating Dutch interference in order to win the

[12] Chapter IV of the present provisional constitution, dealing with the administration of the territories, does little more than state that future arrangements shall be established by law, although it is provided that the territories shall be given the largest possible measure of autonomy to manage their local government and that the principles of consultation and representation shall be considered. The fall of the Natsir cabinet in March 1951 was occasioned largely by disagreement over the mode of election of representative councils for the provinces and other lesser units, indicating a substantial interest in the problem. For a detailed discussion of some of the problems involved, see Lawrence S. Finkelstein, "The Indonesian Federal Problem," *Pacific Affairs*, Sept. 1951, pp. 284–95.

full fruits of a separate national life. In addition it was contended that a poor country, suffering from a critical shortage of trained manpower, could not afford the luxury of a multiplication of governmental structures.

The death of federalism by no means, however, eliminates the need for a constitutional order which will give adequate expression to both the geographic dispersion and the ethnic diversity of the Indonesian people. Even full acceptance of the basic nationalist thesis that the Indonesians constitute one nation from the northern tip of Sumatra to Papua (New Guinea), "from Sabang to Merauke," cannot eliminate the fact that any rigid adherence to a doctrine of centralization would do violence to the differences which inevitably seek some measure of autonomy. There still lies ahead the task of working out the proper forms for a type of autonomy which will give an opportunity for diversity and encourage local participation without at the same time playing into the hands of the separatists or setting up too cumbrous and expensive a hierarchy of political institutions. It is to be hoped that any system which may be devised will not only retain and encourage the democratic cast of government at the lower village level, but will also build on this foundation to spread democracy and effective popular participation upwards to the larger units from this fundamental base. If this is not consciously and deliberately promoted, there is a very real danger that the authoritarian tradition of the past will combine with the present separateness of the dominant elite to produce an over-centralized system which works essentially from the top down.

In all colonial countries coming to independence one of the most difficult issues to be faced is that of finding the men who can take over the management of the new responsibilities which have been assumed, and Indonesia has been peculiarly troubled on this score. Under a colonial regime the upper and controlling posts can be assumed to be occupied almost wholly by the metropolitan power, with the result that the number of nationals of the new state experienced in taking decisions, administering the complex affairs of state, and wielding power is likely to be extremely limited. Beyond this there is the problem of manning the whole network of posts involved in the establishment of a foreign office and representation abroad, including participation in international organizations, not to mention the probable and deeply desired expansion of native participation in the upper ranks of economic life. If to this already large order there be added the need for greatly expanded education and social welfare services, the burden to be carried by the relatively few who are available becomes virtually intolerable.

In the Indonesian case what may be taken as the normal difficulties were enhanced by the small number of those who had received higher education under the Dutch and by the fact that the Eurasians, who were classified as Europeans under the Dutch system and filled a substantial number of the civil service posts in the upper and middle ranges, generally declared for the Dutch and ruled themselves out of the nationalist camp. The consequent drastic shortage of qualified personnel has been and continues to be one of the gravest problems with which the Republic has been faced. It has struggled manfully with it and is striving to multiply the trained reserves on which it can draw but the government has had to operate under a great handicap up to the present time, and many youngsters have had to interrupt their schooling in mid-course to step into posts for which no more mature and trained people were available. It might also be added that the administrative machinery has frequently creaked and suffered from the effects of the provision in the agreements reached at the Hague Conference of 1949 that Dutch civil servants in Indonesia should be maintained in their positions for a period of two years. Given a large stock of good will between the Indonesians and the former colonial power this provision might have served to ease the years of transition, but the legacy of ill will, mutual suspicion, and disputes over such matters as the destiny of New Guinea worked to make the actual relationships unhappy and generally unsuccessful.

On the face of the record as seen from outside, Indonesia has made steady and substantial progress in the extraordinary difficult years leading up to and following independence, but there is evidence which cannot be taken lightly that a pernicious disease has been sapping its vitality internally. In a single phrase this disease can best be identified as a grievous loss of morale which threatens the great gains already achieved. Even more than the strong hold of the Communists in the ranks of organized labor and such more local disturbances as the disaffection in the Moluccas, South Celebes, and Acheh, and the strength of Darul Islam in West Java, this loss of morale works to undercut the effective operation of the democratic institutions which have been established. It is a problem to which President Sukarno, in his role as national watchdog and leader, has made particular and pointed reference in the last year or two, seeing it obviously as a menace which could not be allowed to go unchallenged. In his review on August 17, 1952, of Indonesia's successes and failures in the seven years following the first declaration of independence, the President contrasted in vivid terms the high expectations and ideals of the early revolutionary period with the decay which had more recently set in, and pleaded for a recapture of the earlier fervor and devotion.[13]

"For decades we have longed for our own authority, and now that we have our own authority we do not respect it. . . . All around we see lassitude. All around we see dissatisfaction but without any dynamic positivism. It would ap-

[13] "Indonesia Takes Stock," *Far Eastern Survey*, Oct. 8, 1952, pp. 142–44.

pear almost as if we had no more idealism left. It would appear almost as if we had lost the knack of putting up a struggle in a big way. 'Self interest' would appear to be the enchanting goddess who beckons us in her direction. ..."

Corruption, personal and factional bickering and irresponsibility, and some measure of paralysis of government are the outward symbols of the disease, but it is far too early to conclude that Indonesia is drifting irretrievably downward. The mere fact that Sukarno and others have issued as vigorous and forthright warnings as they have is by itself a sign of health. Furthermore, unless social, political, and moral disintegration has eaten more deeply into the society than seems probable, it is a point of central significance for the future of representative institutions that there is a very wide measure of agreement among the dominant elements as to the general directions of Indonesia's proper course, although the emphasis to be placed on Islam remains to be determined. Leaving aside the extremists of right and left, the bulk of the leadership and of the parties appears to accept with relatively minor variations the two basic propositions that the country should continue to play an independent role in international affairs, aligning itself with neither of the two great blocs, and that it should follow a somewhat left of center economic policy. The drive toward a more rounded economy and the raising of living standards has universal support, and even the differences in emphasis as to the degree of state intervention and participation and the proper role and treatment of foreign enterprise and investment are not strikingly great.[14]

[14] An unusually favorable and optimistic report on the progress of Indonesian affairs is given by Cameron Hawley in "Indonesia: The Fabulous Experiment" (*Harper's Magazine*, August 1954, pp. 36–43), who contends that his observation contradicted the gloomy verdict arrived at by other observers. "The Indonesians," he remarks, "have taught themselves a lot in the last four years. The freedom jag is long over. The hangover aftermath has worn off. Here, to a much greater degree than

A decline in the fervor and devotion which marked the earlier phases of the revolution was inevitable. The problems that lie ahead for Indonesia are to recapture and harness some of the revolutionary spirit to the more humdrum but challenging tasks of constructing a progressive new order, to bring new blood into the ranks of the established leadership, and to make of representative institutions an instrument for the welding together of elite and mass.

---

anywhere else in the countries that fill the globe from Manila to Bombay, I found what impressed me as a realistic approach to the building of a new nation. There is, above all, the realization so rare in Asian countries that building an underdeveloped country into a sound and lasting nation can't be done by magic, fancy ideologies, or foreign aid."

CHAPTER THREE

Burma

OF THE COUNTRIES of Southeast Asia none had gloomier prospects for advance in the immediate postwar years than Burma, but substantial evidence has since accumulated showing that in a quiet and unspectacular way, which compares favorably with any of its neighbors to the east and south, Burma is in fact making significant advances toward its own form of an ordered and progressive democratic society. Devastated in the war, torn by factional dispute and the demands of ethnic minorities, and deprived by one murderous stroke of some of their top leadership, the Burmese have still managed somehow to settle down to business and begin the reconstruction of their country on the basis of a unique combination of Buddhist and Western socialist principles.

The relative success of Burma as an independent republic is all the more surprising in view of the inexperience of its political leaders who had had only some four years of qualified home rule before the country fell to the Japanese and had then demonstrated no outstanding political ability. In addition, the utilization and development of the basically rich resources of the country were gravely hampered by the extensive destruction and disruption caused by the war. Socially, economically, and politically, Burmese development was prejudiced by its close attachment to India, which was arbitrarily instituted from the outset of British rule and lasted until 1937, when Burma was endowed with a constitution of its own and given a large degree of autonomy. Prior to that time the country shared in the constitutional advances and experiments, including dyarchy, which were applied to India and secured a gradually increasing measure of self-government which was regarded as grossly inadequate by the nationalists. Under the Government of India Act of 1935 embodying the new constitution, Burma achieved a modified parliamentary structure which included ministerial responsibility to the lower house of the legislature, although the governor continued to have very extensive reserve and ultimate overriding powers.

The use made by the Burmese of the political opportunities opened to them in 1937 left much to be desired. To an even greater extent in Burma than in other Southeast Asian countries, the political party structure—if indeed it is legitimate to speak of the existence of parties at all at this time—turned out to be a bewildering and rapidly shifting kaleidoscope of factions and personalities with little in the way of a stable base and of coherent and differentiated programs. Charges of corruption and favoritism were widespread, responsible leadership was strikingly absent, and morale fell to a low ebb. In large measure the blame for this state of affairs must be laid at the door of the British, whose policies had in many respects unwittingly served to encourage the disintegration of the older Burmese society and to contribute to the spiritual and even material impoverishment of the Burmese at a time when the economic resources of the country were undergoing rapid expansion. The Burma which Britain ruled has indeed come to be cited as the classic example of the "plural society" in which alien elements are given full play, regardless of the effect on the native inhabitants, and in which the traditional social bonds and restraints are replaced by the stark imperatives of a cash nexus.[1]

[1] The writings of J. S. Furnivall—for example, his *Colonial Policy and Practice* (Cambridge, 1948)—have been the most influential in the elabo-

By the time war in the Far East became a clear possibility the Burmese nationalist leaders were for the most part consumed by a burning hostility to the British, and some among them had already established contact with the Japanese. The advance of Japan's armed forces into Burma was greeted with wide enthusiasm as a means of deliverance from Western imperialism and a Burma Independence Army was organized which gave substantial aid to the invader. The harsh and insolent character of Japanese rule soon dispelled any illusion that real independence was to be achieved under it, even though a formal independence was declared on August 1, 1943. In Burma, as in varying degree in the rest of Southeast Asia, the experience of partial self-government under Japanese auspices proved to be both a further stimulus for nationalism and a valuable training ground for the men who were soon to have full responsibility for the management of their country's affairs. The new government was inevitably in large part a puppet of the Japanese and had to serve their purposes, but it was a Burmese government, operating in the Burmese language and equipped with its own system of courts and a national army. As a recent Burmese government publication puts it:[2]

"Despite the great difficulties, despite the occasional Japanese intervention, Burma was able to show that she could keep up the prestige of the sovereign status she had

---

ration and popularization of this interpretation of Burma's development. Without seeking to question the very great contribution which Mr. Furnivall has made to an understanding both of Burma and, more broadly, of the problems of colonialism, it may legitimately be asked whether he has not overstressed the disintegrating impact of British rule. In view of the achievements of the country since independence and despite the civil wars, it is difficult to evade the conclusion that more in the way of social and cultural cohesion must have been left behind by the British than Mr. Furnivall's drastic analysis would suggest.

[2] *Burma's Fight for Freedom*, Rangoon: Dept. of Information and Broadcasting, Union of Burma, no date, p. 32.

won. From ashes and debris, the structure of freedom slowly rose and shone. The 'independence' was therefore not all 'sham,' not all glitter—there was substance in it, and the glitter, at least a part of it, was the reflection of real gold."

One significant result of the years of occupation was that a substantial reshuffle of political groupings and personalities took place, bringing to the fore a new and largely leftwing coalition known as the Anti-Fascist People's Freedom League (AFPFL) organized in August 1944, which had been shaped as the principal instrument of resistance to the Japanese. Several of the prewar and wartime leaders had either vanished from the scene or been discredited, and among the principal figures in the AFPFL were General Aung San, who headed the national army, and Than Tun, the Communist leader. The British on their return failed signally to recognize the fact that it was a new Burma to which they were coming back, a Burma which had managed to survive for several years without the check or the prop of British civil servants in controlling positions in the administration. On the basis of plans drawn up in India during the war, the British proposed not only no advance over Burma's prewar status but actually something of a retrogression for an interim reconstruction period during which the imperial reins would be held more tightly than before. The promise of a gradual transition to dominion status, perhaps within a period of some six years, was far from adequate compensation for the re-establishment of British rule and for the flat rejection of the AFPFL's demand for a dominant role in the government and a speedy move to independence.[3]

Toward the close of 1946 the deadlock which was thus created was broken by the appointment of a new gover-

[3] For a survey of the developments in the years immediately following the war, see J. S. Furnivall, "Twilight in Burma," *Pacific Affairs*, March and June 1949, pp. 3–20, 155–72.

nor who was prepared to work with Aung San and accept the fact that the AFPFL had a broad base of popular support in the country. Although the domestic situation was complicated by the expulsion from the AFPFL of the Communists, who refused to accept the possibility of negotiations with the British, the drive toward independence found itself within sight of its goal when Prime Minister Attlee announced on December 20 that Burma, like India, could have its independence and invited a Burmese delegation to London to work out plans for self-government either within or outside the Commonwealth. From these conversations in which Aung San took the lead on the Burmese side, there emerged an agreement for Burmese independence as soon as possible and the election of a constituent assembly in April 1947. This assembly, in which the AFPFL held 190 of the 220 seats, soon pronounced for full independence outside the Commonwealth and on September 24 adopted the constitution of the Union of Burma. In the midst of these proceedings, however, Burma was struck a heavy blow when a political rival instigated a gang of gunmen to invade the chambers of the Executive Council in Rangoon and assassinate Aung San and six of his fellow councillors. This shocking loss, which cut deeply into the small number of top-flight Burmese leaders and to which a share of the country's subsequent miseries must be attributed, did not block continued movement ahead. The place of Aung San was taken by Thakin Nu (later known as U Nu), who has remained the principal political figure in Burma since that time, and on October 17, 1947, he and Mr. Attlee signed the agreement providing for complete Burmese independence on January 4, 1948.

Except in relation to the federalist features, which were intended to deal with the troublesome problem of ethnic minorities, the new constitution was closely modeled on the British parliamentary pattern with which the Burmese leaders had become familiar. The place of the king as the formal and symbolic head of the state was taken by a president to be elected by both Chambers of parliament. Although the president's role and powers are described in language not unlike that of his Indonesian counterpart, his actual position in constitutional theory and practice has been far slighter. Whereas Sukarno has held and exercised at least some of the attributes of charismatic leadership with great popular standing and highly significant actual political power, the president of Burma appears rather to have played a dignified and essentially non-political representational role. Effective political leadership has rested with the prime minister and his cabinet, selected by the president on the nomination of, respectively, the Chamber of Deputies and the prime minister himself. In all normal circumstances the substantive powers of the president can be exercised only on the advice of the Union government, headed by the prime minister. If the latter loses the support of a majority in the Chamber, to which the cabinet has collective responsibility, the president may refuse to prorogue or dissolve the Chamber on his advice and must then call upon the Chamber to nominate a new prime minister; if the Chamber fails to come forward with a nomination within fifteen days, it must be dissolved.

Legislative power rests with the parliament in which the Chamber of Deputies plays the principal role but which also contains a Chamber of Nationalities. The former body, which has a normal life of four years and whose membership should be approximately double that of the other Chamber, is elected on a direct basis with special provision for the representation of the Karens. The Chamber of Nationalities consists of 125 members selected to represent the different ethnic elements of the Union, 72 seats being allocated in constitutionally fixed numbers to the Shan, Kachin, and Kayah States, the Special Division of the Chins, and the Karens, the other 53 seats going to the remainder of Burma. The elaborate provisions for the legislative relationship between the two Chambers may be summarized by saying that the Chamber of Deputies has the final word on money bills and that, in case of disagreement on other bills, a joint session of the two Chambers settles the matter by majority vote. An emergency ordinance power, to be exercised when parliament is not in session, is placed in the hands of the president, subject to later parliamentary review.

The federal nature of the Union found original expression in the existence of Shan, Kachin, and Kayah States. A constitutional amendment of 1951, elaborated by further legislation in the succeeding year, made possible the creation of a Karen State as had been foreshadowed in the constitution. The federalism which the constitution envisaged is of a somewhat peculiar variety since the legislative body of each state (the State Council) is composed of that state's representatives in the Chamber of Nationalities, and the executive head of the state is a member of the Union government, bearing the title of Minister for the State in question. His appointment is made by the president on the nomination of the prime minister acting in consultation with the State Council from among the state's members of the Union Parliament. By schedules attached to the constitution a division of legislative competence is made between the central legislature and the State Councils, and a further schedule assigns certain sources of revenue exclusively to the States. Bills passed by a State Council are presented to the president, whose signature appears to be mandatory unless he refers them to the Supreme Court for its decision as to constitutionality. An unusually generous constitutional provision makes it possible for a state to secede from the Union after a lapse of ten years from the date of coming into effect of the constitution, although Section 178 of the constitution denies the right of secession to the Kachin State. The first necessary step for a state which wishes to secede is the adoption of a resolution by at least two-thirds of the total membership of the State Council, which is the signal for the appointment by the president of a plebiscite commission on which the Union and the state have equal representation and which then proceeds to supervise a plebiscite to determine the wishes of the people of the state. It will be of great interest to see, when the appropriate time comes, whether any state chooses to make use of this ultimate right and, if so, whether the dismemberment of the country through secession will in fact be allowed.

Burma is dedicated both by its constitution and by the repeated profession of its leaders to the creation of a progressive and democratic welfare state. The constitution specifies that the sovereignty of the Union resides in the people and all political powers are derived from the people. The fundamental rights of all citizens are laid out in some detail, discrimination against minorities is banned, freedom of religion and conscience is guaranteed although the constitution recognizes the special position of Buddhism as the faith professed by the great majority of Burmese, and constitutional remedies are provided for the safeguard of these rights. As a bulwark for the protection of the individual and the constitutional order, the independence and inviolability of the judiciary was firmly established.

In addition to the classic rights and freedoms the Burmese constitution also goes far in the direction of laying the groundwork for a planned economy on a Socialist model. While the rights of private property and private economic initiative are guaranteed, broad powers are given to the state to intervene both to prevent any use of public property to the detriment of the public interest and to take the lead in the establishment of a more equitable and progressive economic order. The strongly Marxist background of many of the leaders is reflected in such constitutional provisions as those which give the state full control over land ownership, tenure, and distribution and which prohibit large land holdings, "on any basis whatsoever." A recent survey of Burmese affairs suggests that there is a strong affinity between the type of Socialism represented by the present Burmese government and that of Clement Attlee in Great Britain.[4] The Directive Principles of State Policy lay down an impressive body of social welfare goals, look toward the planning of the economic life of the Union with the aim of increasing public wealth and improving the material conditions of the people, and prescribe a policy which shall aim at the operation of public utilities and the exploitation of natural resources by public bodies and co-operatives.

In the case of Burma the provisions of the constitution have been examined in some detail because the subsequent record indicates that the goals which it sets have in fact been the operative principles of the new Burma. Under the chaotic conditions which prevailed in the country during the first years of independence it is obvious that it has not been possible at all times to observe all the constitutional niceties which might have found better expression under other circumstances, but the spirit which lies behind the constitution appears to have reality for those who have had primary responsibility for guiding Burma's course. At the outset the government by no means had control of the whole of the country and there were periods when even its survival in face of the attacks of the insurgents was dubious. In the course of the last two or three years the position of the government has improved very substantially, and by now it may be said that the whole of the country is under control although not all of it is equally securely pacified as yet. The opposition groups made up of Red and White Flag Communists and the PVOS (a sector of the wartime resistance army) remain in the field but their

[4] Frank N. Trager and Helen G. Trager, *Burma: Land of Golden Pagodas*, New York: Foreign Policy Association, Headline Series No. 104, March–April 1954, pp. 32–36.

forces are reduced and their power to do damage lessened.

Another element of opposition to the government which continues active despite military reverses is the organized and militant Karen movement, representing a part but not all of the Karen people who had received preferential treatment under British rule and were disinclined to subordinate themselves to a Burmese government. At the extreme this movement has demanded an independent state which cuts deep into southern Burma, including a large slice of the Irrawaddy delta and embracing areas in which the Karens have only a minority. Both Aung San and U Nu appear to have approached with marked good will the highly difficult problem of working out a settlement with the different ethnic groups which make up a large share of the population of the country, but in the case of the Karens there still remains much to be accomplished.

To an already more than adequately troubled land the movement across the frontier of a substantial body of Chinese Nationalist troops as the Communists took over China added an at least potentially very dangerous irritant. Since the United States was charged with directly or indirectly supporting these troops, the efforts of the government to secure their removal from the country impaired the friendly nature of Burmese-American relations. With the backing of a United Nations General Assembly resolution of 1953 calling for the evacuation or internment of the Chinese troops, a start has been made on clearing up this trouble center and several thousand, but not all, of these troops have been evacuated.

The over-all attitude and policy of U Nu and his associates in the government has been one of meeting force by force where necessary but of seeking at the same time to translate into working reality their aspirations toward democracy and the welfare state. U Nu himself appears to be a man who had political leadership thrust upon him rather than one who went out to seek it. Stepping into the great gap which was left by the assassination of Aung San, he has drawn sustenance from the principles of the Buddhist faith to which he is deeply devoted, and there seems little reason to doubt his professed desire to withdraw from political life rather than to aggrandize his political power and following. The leadership which he has given has been of a quiet and effective variety which has set the tone for a government less afflicted by corruption, favoritism, and other abuses than those of neighboring countries. His position has recently been characterized in the following terms: "Nu of Burma, a schoolteacher by profession, a deeply religious man by preference, is probably closer to the people and has a more immediate appreciation for the peoples of his own and related cultures than any other Asian leader."[5]

An element of stability in the otherwise often confused Burmese political situation has been the clear predominance of the AFPFL, on whose strong majority in the parliament U Nu has been able to base his government. Despite the civil wars which were in progress and which postponed its originally scheduled beginning, a general election was held in successive stages in different regions over a period of half a year, starting in mid-1951. In contrast to Indonesia, which talked of a general election but habitually avoided holding it, the Burmese leaders pushed through the election to generally successful completion except in a relatively small number of areas which remained in the hands of the insurgents. On the whole it was carried off peacefully and although there were some charges of intimidation, tampering with ballot boxes, and other electoral malpractices, there is no reason to doubt that the returns gave a fair approximation of the actual state of public opinion.[6]

[5] Trager, *op. cit.*, p. 18.
[6] *The Economist*, Feb. 9, 1952, pp. 348–50.

The outcome of the election was a sweeping victory for the AFPFL, which won more than three-quarters of the seats, and within the AFPFL the position of the Socialists as the predominant element in the coalition was further strengthened. Other component parts of the coalition are the United Hills Peoples Congress, which draws from the non-Burman peoples other than the Karens; the Union Karen League, which represents non-dissident elements among the Karens; the All Burma Muslim Congress, and the All Burma Youth League. The political opposition—as contrasted with the armed opposition of the Communists and the Karen National Union—is largely of a left-wing variety, even though the governing coalition is itself Socialist, but there are also some right-wing opposition groups which should not be wholly ignored. In this opposition one significant party is the Burma Workers and Peasants Party which split off from the Socialists in 1950 in protest against what was regarded as too friendly a policy toward the West. It has in general taken a position which is barely if at all distinguishable from that of the orthodox Communists, and has sought to build up a coordinated left-wing parliamentary opposition, but it has not been able to achieve as strong a hold among the trade unions as it sought.[7]

Given the Marxist background and leaning of most of the Burmese leaders it is not surprising that since independence the foreign and domestic policy of the country has been strongly pointed leftwards—but not toward Moscow. In the United Nations Burma has consistently been a stalwart member of the Asian-Arab-African bloc and has

[7] For two reviews of Burmese policies and developments, see the articles by E. M. L. Yone and D. G. Mandelbaum in the *Far Eastern Survey*, Oct. 11 and 25, 1950, and Maung Maung, "Burma Looks Ahead," *Pacific Affairs*, March 1952, pp. 40–48. A number of useful and suggestive comments on the constitution and political development of Burma are to be found in Sydney D. Bailey, *Parliamentary Government in Southern Asia* (New York: Institute of Pacific Relations, 1953).

at all times sought to steer a middle course between the great alliances of the super-powers. If it has with some reluctance accepted American aid, it has been insistent that such aid should involve no political or military commitments, and in the spring of 1953, particularly because of the complications raised by the presence in the country of the Chinese Nationalist troops, the government announced that it would accept no further aid from the United States. In many respects, Burma's attitudes and policies bring the country closer to the Western bloc than to the Communists and relations with Great Britain have developed on an amicable basis, but there has been a real effort to build correct and understanding relations with both the Soviet Union and Communist China.

On the domestic score it is one of the striking features of the drive to create a welfare state, based on both Marxist and Buddhist principles, that there has been so significant an attempt to enlist as large as possible a measure of popular understanding and participation. If some of the early pronouncements of the premier and other leaders on such matters as the nationalization of both land and industry gave rise to fears that Burma would utilize its independence to take the plunge over to Moscow's side of the fence, later developments indicate a Socialist policy of considerable moderation and a desire to maintain not only the forms but the substance of democracy as well. Imperialism and the type of capitalist exploitation which is associated with it in the Burmese mind are very firmly ruled out, but there is a readiness to find practical solutions on an undogmatic basis. Buddhism as a creed which serves to moderate Marxist rigidity and intransigence is effective not only for U Nu but for others of the leaders as well. For example, U Ba Swe, in his capacity as President of the Trade Union Congress, has stated that while Marxism and Buddhism are the same in concept, Marxist theory occupies the lower plane of mundane and material affairs whereas Buddhist philosophy is on the higher plane of spiritual liberation; and he added that Burma must develop its own application of Marxism: "Our revolution is entirely Burmese, conforming to Burmese methods and Burmese principles, suitable to Burma."[8]

In its social, economic, and political planning, the government has set itself high and admirable goals and has sought to bring them to the people. Not content with the elaboration of plans at the central national level, U Nu and his associates have made what appear to be determined and concrete efforts to acquaint the general populace with them and to incorporate in them the desires of the villages. As the president of the Union has stated, the Pyidawtha Conference of 1952 prepared a chart for the welfare state, "big in conception and immense in possibilities. It is the duty and privilege of every citizen of the Union to help in the implementation of these schemes. In accordance with the teaching of our Lord Buddha, we must work out our own salvation."[9] In preparation for this conference meetings were held all over Burma, and the conference itself was composed of more than a thousand delegates representing different aspects of Burmese life. In the course of its sessions a series of resolutions were adopted laying out in some detail plans for the reform, democratization, and decentralization of the political and administrative structure, for economic development, land nationalization, and for educational and health development. Among other things the conference provided for the establishment of divisional, district, and township welfare committees, in which representatives of the people as well as officials would participate to develop plans, discuss them with the central authorities, arrange for funds, and assure popular partici-

[8] U Ba Swe, *The Burmese Revolution*, Rangoon: Information Department, Union of Burma, 1952, p. 7.
[9] *Burma: The Fifth Anniversary*, Rangoon: Director of Information, 1953, p. vi.

pation in their execution. In presenting this resolution, the Minister for Public Works and Rehabilitation laid down what seems to be not only a necessary form of words but a working conviction of the present government:[10]

"In a democracy, it is essential that everybody—the people in every village and town, officials at all levels and departments of government and experts and specialists in every field—participates actively in planning and makes his contribution to national welfare and development. Everyone must plan, and no idea or plan must be refused consideration on grounds that it is wild, impractical, or insignificant."

A glowing version of the hopes which center on the Pyidawtha welfare and development projects was contained in a recent Voice of Burma radio broadcast:[11]

"Pyidawtha is all-embracing. All government activities fall neatly within the fold of Pyidawtha. Building railways and roads, bridges and buildings; starting new schools and colleges; opening hospitals and sending out travelling medical vans into remote villages; building factories in the industrialization plan, harnessing rivers to drive the power plants; improving agricultural methods and stepping up production; conducting surveys of the mineral wealth of the country and the engineering prospects—all these and many more come under Pyidawtha. Democratisation of government—that great experiment by which popularly elected councils will learn to look after the affairs of the village and town—is as much an essential part of Pyidawtha as building a sister town to Rangoon to divert the capital's surplus population. The brave new education plans which include free education in schools and at the University levels, mass education, translation and active dissemination through various media—these plans link

[10] *The Pyidawtha Conference: Resolutions and Speeches*, Rangoon: Burmese Ministry of Information, 1952, p. 6.
[11] *Burma* (Information Bulletin of the Embassy of Burma), Washington, D.C., Feb. 15, 1954, p. 10.

with other plans in Pyidawtha. Thus, a critical observer may like to say that Pyidawtha is nothing more than the usual government functions and activities called by a new and fancy name. A conscientious government would have to carry out the programmes anyway, whatever it may choose to call those programmes. So the critic may say.

"That may well be so. But Pyidawtha is not limited to the government; in fact, government is but one of the agencies through which Pyidawtha gets things done. The main motive power that drives the projects comes from the peoples themselves. It is true that the ideas and the general guidance come from the government and other circles, but once the ideas have caught on with the peoples it is they who sweep forward in a great upsurge of enthusiasm.

"Pyidawtha is also a social revolution in this sense; for the first time in history, government officials are taking to the field to help the villagers mend their roads, dig their wells, build their bridges, to help them in building a brave new life."

It need scarcely be said that it is improbable that Burma will now or in the foreseeable future achieve the full limits of the ideals it has set for itself, but there is no reason to assume that the economic goals which have been established cannot be realized within a generation or so, unless grave and unpredictable interruptions intrude themselves. Burma, however, remains a country which cannot be held to be beyond the potentiality of serious civil disturbance, and its experience of modern democratic government is sharply limited. As in other countries of Southeast Asia its resources in trained manpower are exceedingly meager—a shortcoming which cannot help but have a drastic effect on the ability to establish and manage the welfare state to which it is dedicated. There is in Burma as elsewhere the always dangerous cleavage between the Western-educated, Western-oriented leadership and the peasant mass, but the strong hold of Buddhism and the apparent readiness of the leaders to seek contact with the grass roots may aid in bridging the gap. It may be added that in the opinion of some qualified observers the distance between rural and urban groups, between well-off and not-so-well-off, is less in Burma than in any country of South and Southeast Asia, and as in the case of Thailand the existence of ample supplies of rice aids in checking discontent. The country has succeeded in balancing its budget and its international financial and trade position is strong, even though neither its rice exports nor its economic life in general have yet reached the prewar level.

The spirit and the achievements of the Burma of the last few years give substance to the conclusion of Justice William O. Douglas: "It is clear, however one views the Welfare State of Burma, that it offers a democratic, not a Communist, answer to the problems of feudal Asia."[12]

[12] William O. Douglas, *North from Malaya*, New York, 1953, p. 253.

CHAPTER FOUR

Malaya

OF THE COUNTRIES of Southeast Asia, Malaya, divided into the two governmental units of Singapore and the Federation of Malaya, is the only one which has retained its full colonial status even though the heavy hand of colonialism has been by no means wholly removed from Indochina. The continuance of the colonial regime has combined with Malaya's peculiar internal difficulties to keep the country's parliamentary institutions at an embryonic level despite the substantial advance which has been made since the war in political structure and even more in the growth of political consciousness. At every turn the country is bedeviled by a racial problem as close to insoluble as any that exists in the world. To the complications created by the diversities of race, language, religion, and culture there is added the fact that for many of Malaya's inhabitants, and particularly for the Chinese, there cannot help but be doubt as to the extent of their loyalty to and identification with the country of their adoption. If there is much talk of nationalism, there are still no more than the faintest rudiments of a single Malayan nation. Leaving wholly aside the reluctance of the British to press for political advance in an area so vital as a dollar earner and as a strategic center, it is still very difficult to envisage the successful establishment of a democratic system based on representative government. In one form or another the experiment must be tried, but experience elsewhere encourages no great hope that parliamentary institutions can operate effectively where there is so little homogeneity and so meager a popular sense of sharing in a common destiny.

The headlines of recent years have been occupied by the Communist guerrilla warfare, locally known as the Emergency and bearing its own close relation to the communal problem, but the probability is that this bitter and destructive struggle will have vanished from the scene long before it has been possible to dispose of the more fundamental ills of perhaps the most incurably plural of all plural societies. In the prewar decades these ills could be relatively easily ignored or evaded in view of the considerable prosperity of the country, the general political apathy and indifference, and the readiness of the populace in most of its segments to take British rule for granted and let the future take care of itself. In the postwar period the basic discords have thrust themselves into the foreground and demand drastic action even though there are few who would dare to claim that they can confidently name the answers. To diagnose the malady is not difficult; to know how to deal with it within the limits of the time and means available is a very different story.

Any consideration of Malaya's political prospects must set off from the bare demographic facts of the country, which can be most conveniently presented in tabular form:[1]

	Malaysians	Chinese	Indians	All others	Total
Singapore	127,063	806,690	75,601	32,579	1,041,933
Federation	2,631,154	2,043,971	586,371	75,726	5,337,222
Total	2,758,217	2,850,661	661,972	108,305	6,379,155

[1] These figures are drawn from the *Annual Reports* for Singapore and the Federation for 1951. The term "Malaysian" is used to include not only the older established Malays of the peninsula but also the relatively large number of persons of kindred stocks from Indonesia who have come to the country in recent times.

In Malaya as a whole the two major races are approximately in balance, but it is obvious that the separation of Singapore from the mainland has served to give the Malays of the Federation only a slim numerical predominance over the Chinese and has left them, by a hair's breadth, with less than half of the total population. The unadorned figures themselves present the heart of the story but there are many other aspects which must be taken into account. Although the Malays, aside from the relatively small number of aborigines, may presumably be taken as the native inhabitants of the country, the greater part of its wealth and development must be attributed to the skill and industry of the later immigrants. A decade or two ago the claims of the latter might with some plausibility have been dismissed or at least discounted by the contention they were on the whole only temporary migrants whose basic national attachments lay elsewhere. Since the depression, however, and particularly since the start of the second World War, immigration has come to a virtual halt and the turnover in population is a fragment of its earlier dimensions. A single comparison adequately illustrates the point: of the total Chinese population in Malaya in 1921 only 22 percent were born in the country, whereas the census of 1947 revealed that in that year the figure had risen to 62.5 percent. However strong the temptation may be to condemn the British for instigating and encouraging the great influx of Chinese and Indians who have tended to submerge the Malays in their own country, the stark fact remains that they are there, are presumably there to stay, and must be taken into account in any effort to produce a viable political system.

Given a foundation of real good will and devotion to a common cause it might be possible to envisage harmonious self-government developing for such a heterogeneous assemblage, but good will and mutual devotion are notoriously lacking. To the Chinese the Malays appear as an indolent and backward people who have not only been unduly protected by the British but also arbitrarily endowed with such political power as the British have not reserved for themselves. To the Malays the Chinese appear as alien intruders who at the best have only partially severed their connections with China, who have exploited the country and its people, deliberately excluding the Malays from economic life, and who now seek to rival the Malays in the political sphere as well. The rise of political consciousness and activity, far from uniting the several races of Malaya as a single nation struggling for independence, has so far served rather to divide and to sharpen racial antagonisms.

It cannot be said that British rule of Malaya has done much to unify the country's peoples—although any honest analyst of the situation must admit that it is far simpler to attack what the British have done than to produce alternative policies which would have had significantly different results. Generally speaking, at least until the outbreak of the war, the British were content to follow any line of policy which speeded the development of the country and maintained the peace. The Malays were in a sense given a favored position in that they were protected in their land holding, their sultanates were maintained, and they were given some access to the civil service, but precisely this measure of special privilege preserved them from the necessity of making any strenuous effort to adapt themselves to the exigencies of the modern world. The Chinese, on the other hand, although they were generally excluded from political participation, were given free rein in the economic sphere and made the best of it. In the prewar world this version of a plural society was not very difficult to keep in balance. The Malays were generally content with things as they were and failed to take adequate notice of the fact that their country was slipping from their grasp, while neither the Chinese nor the Indians demonstrated enough interest in the political affairs of Malaya to cause serious disturbance. Aside from a not very vociferous Communist fringe, primarily limited to the Chinese, and occasional flurries of excitement concerned rather with the national movements in their own countries than with Malayan politics, the two major non-Malay communities were prepared to accept the fact of British rule without significant protest. Under the surface new and disruptive forces were at work, but up to the outbreak of the war Britain could manage the Malayan society without any important breach with the old-established colonial techniques. If there was considerable talk of the need for affirmative action to weld the different races together, very little in fact was done which went beyond keeping the peace between communities which for the most part went their separate ways.

The Japanese occupation put an end to an old era, but its effect in producing a new one was less clear than elsewhere. The defeat of the British, the collapse of the invincible fortress of Singapore, and the arrival of new masters had the same type of impact in some respects as on the rest of Southeast Asia, but the Malayan society was both too immature and too divided to allow the consolidation of a national movement which could take over when the day of the Japanese had ended. Instead of consolidation the Japanese in fact brought to life the communal hostilities latent in the country since the Malays tended to accept the new regime complacently whereas the Chinese were persecuted and antagonistic, and the Indians woke to a new sense of their political potentialities. The resistance movement was very largely a Chinese affair in which the Communists played a leading role, and it left behind it not only the customary heritage of violence and bitterness but also a body of Chinese squatters who had retreated to the jungle and later contributed greatly to the guerrilla activities of the Emergency.

The return of the British to this disrupted country was

accepted with pleasure or at least with equanimity in many quarters, although it was not long before trouble of various kinds broke loose. The British brought with them plans for a new order which had been worked out in London during the war and which looked toward a radical rationalization of the political set-up. The two major features of the new order were a re-alignment of political units in such fashion as to establish Singapore as a colony by itself and the joining of Penang and Malacca with the former Federated and Unfederated Malay States to form a Malayan Union in which the jurisdiction of the Sultans gave way to the jurisdiction of the British Crown. The official British statement of policy[2] concerning the future constitution emphasized the fact that while the prewar divisions and separations within a little country were not inappropriate to its stage of development at that time,

"the increasing complexity of modern administrative, economic and social developments demand a system of government less cumbersome, more adequate for large common services, and making better use of time and labour. . . . A stage has now been reached where the system of government should be simplified and reformed. . . . On a longer view, too, the prewar system will not lend itself to that political adjustment which will offer, through broadbased institutions in which the whole community can participate, the means and prospect of developing Malaya's capacity in the direction of responsible self-government. In this development all those who have made the country their homeland should have the opportunity of a due share in the country's political and cultural institutions. Efficiency and democratic progress alike demand therefore that the system of government should be simplified and reformed.

"The British Crown must provide the common link which will draw together the communities of Malaya and

[2] Cmd 6724, Jan. 1946.

promote a sense of common interest and the development of common institutions."

In order to achieve the participation of the whole community in the new broad-based institutions, there was furthermore provision for the creation of a common citizenship of the Malayan Union which would have had the effect of bestowing political rights on the great bulk of the non-Malay inhabitants of the Union.

It is arguable that the British once having taken this plunge into drastic reform and modernization would have been well advised to stand by it,[3] but the storm of Malay indignation, backed by the protests of a number of the pro-Malays among the British, brought it to an end before it was properly started. It was the Malay contention that the revision of treaties with the Malay Rulers which had been undertaken was improper in form and content, that the Sultans and the Malay people in general had been pushed too low down in the scale, and that the Chinese had been raised too high. The position of the proponents of the scheme was weakened by the fact that the Chinese, although they were presumably the principal beneficiaries, failed to produce the political backing for it which might have been expected, and the British no doubt suffered some pangs of conscience from the charge that they were violating the obligations which they had earlier assumed in relation to the Rulers and their people. At all events, the venture was shortly abandoned and was replaced by a Federation of Malaya which restored the jurisdiction of the Sultans and came nearer to being an approximation of the old balance between the races.

Prewar Malaya knew little of democracy. "The Governor had almost absolute authority in the Straits Settle-

[3] A somewhat different estimate of the situation is contained in the comment by S. W. Jones that "the best that could be said for the proposals of the Colonial Office was that at a later date they might be proved right." *Public Administration in Malaya*, London and New York, 1953, p. 138.

ments and the advice of the Residents and Advisers in the States had to be accepted on all matters except religion. ... Both in the British and in the Malay structure, government was from the top down, and did not afford expression of the people's will through their own chosen representatives.... In practise, legislation in both the States and the Colony was formulated, introduced and made law by British officials."[4] In the legislative councils the timehonored Crown Colony device of an official majority guaranteed the predominance of the official view although public sentiment could make itself felt to some degree through the appointed unofficial members. The absence of any system for the election of representatives was dictated not only by the convenience of British officialdom but also by the very real difficulty of discovering an electorate which might properly be enfranchised. Furthermore, in the Malay States the British paid something more than lip service to the contention that sovereignty remained vested in the Sultans who had accepted British protection, although they were not unaware of the useful cover the Sultans provided them. There can be no answer to the question as to whether the British might have won more in the way of popular loyalty and brought the races somewhat closer together if they had ventured on a bolder policy of political advance; but the record is clear that they were under no pressure to do so from any significant segment of the population.

Much the same question can be asked, but with a less academic flavor, about the present situation. In the years since the end of the war Britain has edged cautiously toward the grant of a greater measure of representative institutions,[5] but there is still a large gap between the

[4] John F. Cady, Patricia G. Barnett, and Shirley Jenkins, *The Development of Self-Rule and Independence in Burma, Malaya and the Philippines*, New York, 1948, pp. 55–57.

[5] A concise description of the constitutional developments in Malaya since the war can be found in Jones, *op. cit.*, Chap. X.

existing systems and the self-government which has been promised for the future. As far as the elective principle is concerned, Singapore has moved ahead more rapidly than the Federation where the Emergency and the more intense communal problem were drawn upon as justification for making haste slowly. New constitutional arrangements adopted in 1954 for both areas introduced drastic changes of a democratic variety.

In keeping with developments elsewhere in the colonial empire, the postwar constitutions of both Singapore and the Federation provided for the introduction of unofficial majorities in the Legislative Councils. At the time of the 1954 reforms the Legislative Council of Singapore consisted of the Governor as president, nine members of the official hierarchy, four nominated unofficial members, and twelve elected members, three of whom were elected by the Singapore, Chinese, and Indian Chambers of Commerce respectively, and the remainder by popular vote based on a limited franchise which provided an electorate of only some 48,000 for the 1951 election.

The Federation's Legislative Council of seventy-five members was three times as large as that of Singapore but its unofficial contingent of fifty had a less direct relation to the people since none of its members were elected but were appointed to represent a specified list of interests and communities.[6] The highly diversified list of "interests, groups, and activities" which secured representation included labor, the major divisions of economic life, professional, educational and cultural interests, and the Eurasian, Ceylo-

[6] A dim view of the Council, as of a number of other aspects of contemporary Malaya, is taken by Francis G. Carnell in a vigorous article, "Communalism and Communism in Malaya," *Pacific Affairs*, June 1953. He compares it to the consultative councils of corporate states and protests that while ninety percent of the people of the country are peasants or small wage earners, the Council is ninety percent middle class in composition, comprising "mainly senior British and Malay civil servants, wealthy Chinese lawyers and businessmen, and Europeans representing the powerful planting and mining interests."

nese, Indian, and Chinese communities. In the determination of the membership of the Council one of the aims was to secure "a slight preponderance of Malays over non-Malays" since "His Majesty's Government recognize that the Malays certainly form an absolute majority amongst those in the country who regard Malaya as their permanent home and the object of their loyalty."[7] As far as the body of unofficial members was concerned, it was presumed that, although the main principle of allocation was non-communal in character, the Malays would have twenty-five seats, the Chinese fifteen, Europeans seven, Indians five, and Ceylonese and Eurasians one each. In addition to the unofficial contingent the Council was rounded out in the customary British colonial pattern by the membership of fourteen officials plus the presidents of each of the nine State Councils and two members selected by the Councils of Penang and Malacca.

A move in the general direction of more full-fledged parliamentary institutions was made early in 1951 through the introduction of the so-called "Member" system which began to give the Executive Council, now consisting of twenty-one members under the presidency of the High Commissioner, something of the look of a cabinet. The Deputy High Commissioner, Chief Secretary, Attorney General, and Financial Secretary continued to sit *ex officio*, and some posts, such as those of the Secretaries of Defense and Chinese Affairs and the Members for Economic Affairs and for Industrial and Social Relations, were placed in the hands of officials. In the case of other departments, however, the official departmental head was replaced by an unofficial Member, appointed by and responsible to the High Commissioner, who became the political head of the department and its spokesman in the

[7] *Federation of Malaya: Summary of Revised Constitutional Proposals*, Cmd 7171, p. 7. The allocation of the unofficial seats is given on the same page.

Legislative Council. The departments thus transferred to unofficial leadership include Home Affairs, Health, Education, Agriculture and Forestry, and Lands, Mines and Communications. The unofficial Members appointed at the inauguration of the new plan were three Malays, one Ceylonese, and one European. The Member system was obviously only a partial step not only because a number of the key posts remained in official hands but also because there was no elected legislature to which the Members might owe the usual ministerial responsibility, but it prepared the way for more far-reaching changes. In its present form it gives a greater opportunity to a few political leaders to influence policy and gain experience than was possible under the prior arrangements and also serves to make somewhat easier the task of securing support for governmental measures in a necessarily inchoate legislature, now endowed with a more direct stake in the executive branch of the government. A further step in advance, hailed by General Templer as "a sign post on the road of political progress," came in 1953 when the High Commissioner withdrew from his role as president of the Legislative Council and the Council installed as its own Speaker a Malay who had previously been Mentri Besar of Pahang, a member of the Council since its inauguration, and also Member for Lands, Mines, and Communications.

The next major step toward representative institutions in the Federation must obviously be the extension of elections to cover the array of councils already in existence at various levels. The British program in this connection was laid out at some length by the High Commissioner in an address to the Legislative Council in November 1952:[8]

---

[8] *Malaya: General Templer Reviews Progress*, Washington, D.C.: British Information Services, Dec. 11, 1952, p. 6. See also Gerald Hawkins, "First Steps in Malayan Local Government," *Pacific Affairs*, June 1953, pp. 155–58.

"Honourable Members will remember that in my inaugural address I used the analogy of a house. I said that we were not going to put on the roof until the foundations were truly laid and until the uprights were firmly in position. The Local Councils Ordinance establishes widespread training grounds in rural areas for the practice of the basic principles of democratic Government, in the use of electoral machinery, and in the exercise of personal and corporate responsibility. By the end of this year, it is expected that over one hundred areas will have been gazetted as Local Council Areas, and many of their Councils will have been elected in time to prepare their first budgets for the financial year beginning on the 1st January, 1953. We can fairly claim, therefore, that at least the foundations of the house have been laid and are beginning to set properly. Seventeen towns with populations of over 10,000 people are to have Town Councils with a majority of elected members by the second half of 1953, according to present indications. These will be in addition to the elected Municipal Councils of Penang, Malacca, and Kuala Lumpur. The next phase in the building program will be the erection of the uprights, that is to say, the creation of elected State and Settlement Councils. I have reason to hope that at least one of these corner posts will be in position early in 1954, but as I said last March, it is folly to build upon sand, and to proceed with the superstructure before the foundations are well and truly laid."

As this programmatic speech explicitly states, it was the intention of General Templer to make haste slowly, and it will be noted that there is no direct mention of the Federal Legislative Council, which presumably constitutes the ultimate roof. While an admirable theoretical case can be made for the argument that political experience and free institutions must grow from the ground up, it is a far more dubious proposition that in the ferment of present-day Malaya it is possible to proceed with such slow and majestic deliberation.

One of the bitterest critics of General Templer and the recent policies of the British Government has put the matter in the following terms:[9]

"Only an independent, self-respecting Malaya with a will to defend itself from any outside interference can deal effectively with the Communist threat, and toward this end no effective progress is being made. In official propaganda great play is made of democratic elections to the town councils, whereas, in fact, a city like Kuala Lumpur, with a population of nearly 300,000, has an electoral roll of only about 7,000. The vast majority of the Kuala Lumpur ratepayers, who are mainly Chinese, are disenfranchised under the Selangor local-government law. The new 'village councils' are scarcely more representative than the town councils and have fewer powers. The so-called 'Member System' is held out to be a first step towards a kind of cabinet government, but unlike Ministers in the Gold Coast and Nigeria, for example, the 'Members' in Malaya are in no way responsible to the Legislature which remains entirely nominated. Moreover, the MCA-UMNO alliance, the most powerful political force in the country, was, until late in 1953, entirely unrepresented. Even now it has only two of the quite arbitrarily selected eleven Members. . . . Malaya early in 1954 is politically one of the most backward territories in the British Empire."

That the government itself was coming to a growing awareness of the needs and pressures was indicated by the High Commissioner's creation in the summer of 1953 of a committee of forty-six members to report to the Legislative Council on the question of elections to the Council, including in its terms of reference the recommendation of constitutional changes in the Federal government arising from elections. The appointment of this committee followed a flurry of political activity which came to involve all the

[9] Victor Purcell, *Malaya: Communist or Free?* London and Stanford, 1954, p. 7.

politically significant elements of Malaya in the process of working out new constitutional arrangements.[10]

The first program to be put forward was one which had been worked out early in 1953 by the alliance, commented on below, of the two major communal organizations, the United Malays National Organization and the Malayan Chinese Association. In March this alliance announced its agreement on the principle of general elections for the Council. In the first week of April UMNO approved this agreement which called for a three-fifths elected Council of seventy-five members, only thirty-one of whom would be nominated. A resolution calling for Federal elections by 1954 was unanimously adopted, and a further resolution ominously proposed that if the government rejected the program, the representatives of the alliance should resign their seats in the Council.

This move was shortly countered by a group consisting largely of somewhat more conservative or traditionally oriented Malays, headed by seven Mentris Besar of the Malay States, who organized a National Conference which proceeded to appoint a working committee to look into the constitutional problem. Although the United Malays National Organization and the Malayan Chinese Association were invited to join the Conference they did not attend, but there was a sprinkling of representatives from the several races of Malaya. The report of the working committee, adopted by the Conference at a second meeting on August 31, looked to a gradualist program of advance of which the first stage should be completion of elections to State and Settlement Councils by 1955, to be followed in the succeeding year by the addition of some elected members to the Federal Council. The Conference explicitly took the position that Malaya was not yet ready

[10] For an account of these developments, see Francis G. Carnell, "Constitutional Reform and Elections in Malaya," *Pacific Affairs*, Sept. 1954, pp. 216–35. A convenient summary of some of the proposals which were put forward is given in *Venture*, Nov. 1953, p. 10.

for an elected Council and that it would be a "mockery of democracy" to seek to impose elections immediately. It was further proposed that the Executive Council should contain only holders of portfolios as the next step toward an effective system of cabinet government.

In the course of the summer the UMNO-MCA alliance, not to be outdone, also called a National Convention which elaborated and formally adopted the program which had been put forward in the spring. This program, which claimed to have the endorsement of "all the democratic Malayan political parties," continued to call for Federal elections in 1954 as the first step in the attainment by peaceful and constitutional means of sovereign and independent statehood within the British Commonwealth. A more detailed proposal was presented in October by a working committee of the National Convention which suggested that Malaya should take the constitution of the Gold Coast as its model and move immediately to a legislative assembly of which the majority would be elected. It also recommended that the Executive Council should have a majority of members chosen from the elected members of the assembly and approved by majority vote of the latter. An even larger elected majority in the Council was called for by the proposal of a newcomer in the political field, the Pan-Malayan Labour Party, which backed the demand for elections in 1954.

On January 31, 1954, the official committee appointed by the High Commissioner issued its report which represented principally the labors of a working party of nineteen members under a British chairman with ten Malays and three members each from the British, Indian, and Chinese communities. This committee unanimously opposed election of all members of the Legislative Council for present purposes, contending that the political and economic life of the country had not yet developed to a point where a full system of elections could adequately represent it. A four year transitional period was suggested after which the situation should again be reviewed in the light of the experience gained. The committee was, however, split on the balance to be maintained in the interim between the elected and the nominated members of the Council, a substantial majority favoring a slight predominance of nominated members and a minority asking that sixty members of the Council be elected as against forty to be nominated. Under both the majority and the minority proposals the Council's membership was to be enlarged and a strong representation of so-called scheduled interests, largely economic in character, was to be continued. Other provisions of the report called for direct election by territorial constituencies on a non-communal basis, with a franchise unlimited by literacy or property requirements. As a hesitant step in the direction of responsible government the report suggested that the High Commissioner should consult the majority in the legislature before proceeding to the appointment of members of the Executive Council.

Although the views expressed by the majority in the report were accepted in some circles as representing an adequate advance for the time being, the UMNO-MCA alliance, the Pan-Malayan Labour Party, and other groups received the report with open hostility. The alliance, whose political strength was unquestionably considerable, declared its unreadiness to accept the postponement of elections beyond November 1954, a reduction in its proposal for an elected three-fifths majority, and the recommendation in the report that government officials should not be allowed to stand for election—a provision of particular concern to the Malays. Indeed, the alliance now went beyond its original demands and asked for a fully elected legislature. When the Colonial Secretary, Oliver Lyttelton, refused to receive a delegation sent to London by the alliance in April 1954, one of the leaders of the delegation, Sir Cheng-lock Tan, was reported to ask whether the people of Malaya would demand their political freedom or remain like dumb, driven cattle: "The age of empire is at an end. But we are still slaves politically and legally and we hold our liberty on sufferance to our masters."

Whether because of pressure from the alliance and its backers or for other reasons, the decision of the government was to reject the majority report. Following consultations between the High Commissioner, the Malay Rulers, and the authorities in London, a White Paper was issued in Kuala Lumpur on April 27 which set the composition of the Council at fifty-two elected members and forty-six appointed, with elections slated for the succeeding year. An elected majority was thus secured, but it still fell short of the three-fifths originally demanded by the alliance. Its leaders have not only threatened to boycott the forthcoming elections, but have also carried out their threat to withdraw alliance representatives from the Council when it met in June. Although it is unlikely that the government will yield further a potentially dangerous situation has been created.

Shortly after the appearance of this report on the Federation's legislature, a Commission headed by Sir George Rendel put forward more radical proposals for the reform of the constitution of Singapore. Although the Commission rejected the argument for "almost complete independence for Singapore forthwith" on the ground that too hurried an emancipation might in fact work to bring about a Communist dictatorship, it recommended both a heavy predominance of elected members in the legislative assembly and a decided move in the direction of cabinet government. For the legislature it proposed an increase from the present twenty-five members to thirty-two, of whom twenty-five would be elected, three would serve *ex-officio,* and four would be nominated unofficials. More than a little heartburning was caused in interested quarters by the proposal that the members hitherto stemming from the Chambers of Commerce should be abolished, although the Chambers would be represented in a new Trade Advisory Council. The existing Executive Council, it was recommended, should give way to a Council of Ministers to consist of three official members (the Chief Secretary, Financial Secretary, and Attorney General) and six members selected from the assembly on the recommendation of the leader of the largest party or of a coalition able to secure majority support. The ministers would head executive departments, be responsible for "determination of policy in all matters other than those relating to external affairs, internal security, and defense," have collective ministerial responsibility, and in effect perform "all the duties normally performed by the cabinet in a fully self-governing state." Recognizing the failure of the system of voluntary registration of voters, the Commission proposed the adoption of a system of automatic registration in order to secure a larger electorate. Despite strong representations to the contrary, it was recommended that English should remain the official language of the Colony and the only language to be used in the legislative assembly. Reforms in the structure of the local government were also proposed by the Commission.[11]

[11] *The Times* (London), Feb. 25, 1954. An interesting series of proposals in relation to the reform of the Singapore constitution were laid before the Rendel Commission by the Council of Joint Action which purports to represent twenty thousand government employees. The Council's views were presented to the Commission at a meeting attended by seven hundred of its members. In addition to proposals which were accepted in substance by the Commission, the Council asked that the restriction on the use of other languages than English be dropped in order to allow of more effective representation for the large majority of non-English speaking elements in the population, the use of trade-union funds in elections, and the participation in political life of civil servants. The latter point had also been argued in the Federation with special reference to the fact that many of the Malays equipped with a modern type of education would be found in the government service and that the Malay community would be placed at a disadvantage if they could not play a political role. The Council also suggested

Those who are pressing for greater speed in the introduction of the elective principle at all levels in Malaya appear usually to base their arguments on three major contentions, apart from the general virtue of replacing colonialism by democratic self-government. In the first place it is held essential under present Malayan conditions to meet the challenge of Communism not only militarily but also through political reforms which will associate the general populace more closely with the administration and increasingly make the latter an instrument of the popular will. Secondly, it is argued—perhaps over-optimistically—that elections on a non-communal basis will serve to bring the divergent peoples of Malaya together, focus attention on issues which cut horizontally across the vertical barriers of race and religion, and thus become a key part of the program for the vitally necessary building of a Malayan nation. Thirdly, there is a substantial body of critics of the powers-that-be in Malaya who contend that the Malayan elements which have so far been encouraged to come to prominence and power in the Federation represent primarily and almost exclusively the feudal and well-to-do groups whose deadening and communally divisive hold can only be broken, short of a Communist take-over, by an effective appeal to the mass of the people. This latter position is strongly stated in a recent Fabian Colonial Bureau Pamphlet which comments as follows on the still powerful position of the Sultans:[12]

"They are normally responsible to legislative councils of which there is one in each of the nine States. But these legislatures are entirely appointed by the Sultans and consist mainly of Malay court politicians, with feudal back-

---

that there should be no nominated members in the legislature and that the responsibility for internal security should be vested in the hands of a minister coming from the assembly and not in an official. *Straits Times* (Singapore), Jan. 15, 1954.

[12] Derrick Sington, *Malayan Perspective*, London, 1953, p. 8.

grounds, or selected Chinese or Indians who are faithful supporters of sultanate rule.

"Clearly this political structure with its nine poles terminating in feudal oligarchies—which reinforce communal tension—needs to be modified as rapidly as possible. In a country the size of England with a population of six millions these nine components should ultimately become, at the most, provinces or counties. But as long as the Sultans, with their vested interest in the status quo, are allowed—in the name of the Malays—a virtual veto on constitutional change such reforms will be impossible. The aim must be to change the pattern of power in the Malay States themselves.

"The first and obvious way to do this is by transforming the State Councils into elected bodies. . . . Conditions in Malaya are far less disturbed than in Burma where nation-wide elections have already been held. Opposition to elections in the predominantly Malay States is a symptom of clinging to power by the existing sultanate oligarchies. The Malay States are conspicuously backward even in holding elections in the Malay villages."

It is difficult to draw any clear moral from the elections which have so far taken place in Malaya. The electorates remain small and although the number of those actually voting has increased there does not appear to have been any very wide public interest in the proceedings. In the Federation the fact that the elections have been limited to the local level and to councils whose functions are both scanty and unexciting inevitably detracts from their importance in the eyes of the politically active who, whatever the proper theory may be as to the significance of local institutions, look to the central legislature and executive as the real seat of power and decision. For the future of the country it is, however, encouraging both that general and not communal electorates have been created and that communalism has played a substantially smaller role than might have been expected. In the predominantly Chinese city of Singapore the success of Indian candidates, in part reflecting the aroused political consciousness of this community and perhaps also their greater familiarity with electoral procedures, has been particularly striking. In the election of 1948, which was notable as the first election to be held in Malaya, three of the six seats to be filled were won by Indians, the other three going to a Chinese, a European, and a Malay. In the second Legislative Council election of 1951, under somewhat changed ground rules, the Chinese did better, winning three of the nine seats then available, but Indians again also won three, and the remainder went to a European, a Eurasian, and a Ceylonese. Neither of the two parties which entered the second election—Progressive and Labour—looks to a communal base. This demonstrated ability to cut across communal lines is a healthy sign, although the relatively poor showing of the Chinese must be attributed at least in part to their widespread political indifference and apathy under present circumstances as well as to the restrictive character of the franchise.[13]

The political problems of communalism in the Federation are markedly more intense and complex than those of Singapore because the mainland of the peninsula is the stronghold of the Malays which has been invaded in force by Chinese and Indians. Such efforts as have been made to bring about a Malayan unity have to date been

[13] A number of Chinese are excluded from the franchise under the present regulations which are laid out as follows by the *Annual Report* for Singapore for 1951: "To qualify for the Legislative Council register a man or woman must be a British citizen over 21 years of age; must not have taken any steps to acknowledge 'allegiance, obedience or adherence to any foreign power or State,' or held office during the past 3 years under the government of any foreign power, or hold a foreign passport; and must have resided in the Colony for the past 3 years.

"Qualifications for the City Council franchise are similar, but with certain additional residential or property qualifications."

The same Report stated that the electorate for the 1951 Legislative Council election stood at 48,155, with 52 percent of this number actually **voting.**

largely ineffective. The two major political organizations which, aside from the Communists, have come to play the largest role in the last few years are the United Malays National Organization (UMNO) and the Malayan Chinese Association (MCA), and both, as their names indicate, are communal bodies although occasional efforts have been made to broaden their membership on an interracial basis. The Independence of Malaya Party (IMP), founded in 1951 as a non-communal organization seeking self-government within the Commonwealth within a decade, has so far achieved relatively little success, and budding labor parties are still in the early stages of formation.

UMNO is the principal survivor of a number of Malay parties, some with varying degrees of a Communist tinge in the immediate post-liberation period, which sprang up after the war primarily in protest against the Malayan Union scheme which the returning British authorities brought with them.[14] The central figure in its creation and its first president was Dato Onn bin Jaafar, Prime Minister of Johore, who later became Member for Home Affairs in the Federation and has been clearly the outstanding Malay political leader. The political positions which UMNO has taken from time to time have varied, but it is always subject to the temptation to tie itself over-closely to the Sultans and their feudalistic entourage and to the existing State structure, thus making itself effectively an ally of reactionary and communally inclined forces rather than an instrument of adaptation to a new Malayan order. Although UMNO was founded in 1946, its Chinese counterpart, the MCA, did not come into existence until 1949 despite Chinese resentment at the pro-Malay turn of British policy which substituted the Federation for the

[14] For a history and analysis of party and other political developments in Malaya, see T. H. Silcock and Ungku Abdul Aziz, "Nationalism in Malaya," in *Asian Nationalism and the West*, edited by William L. Holland, New York, 1953.

Union under Malay pressure. Presumably the major factor in its creation was the new situation which appeared when the Communists retired to the jungle in 1948 and took up guerrilla warfare, forcing the Chinese community to undertake a re-appraisal of its position. The role which Dato Onn played for the Malays has been played for the Chinese by Tan Cheng Lock, later knighted, and the two leaders have collaborated at many points, as, for example, in the Communities Liaison Committee which has probably been the most important agency working for unity on a non-communal Malayan basis. That there is still much to be desired in the way of intercommunal collaboration, even at this top level, is sharply indicated by the fears expressed by Dato Onn in a speech in Kuala Lumpur early in 1953:[15]

"The Chinese Chambers of Commerce in Malaya are taking the place of the Kuomintang. The Malayan Chinese Association is dominated by the Chinese Chambers of Commerce. . . . I feel really alarmed, because I see, not the wish to build a united, free, independent Malaya, but the wish to build the twentieth province of China."

In 1950–51 Dato Onn's inability to secure a bridging of the communal gap within and through UMNO or other existing bodies led him to break away from UMNO and found the IMP, but this organization has not achieved the position as the crystallizing center of a new non-communal political movement. Indeed, apparently primarily because of the potential threat of the new organization,

[15] *The Times* (London), March 26, 1953. Dato Onn also suggested that the Chinese Chambers of Commerce were taking on the role of Chinese consulates.

It has, incidentally, been a matter of some comment that Communist China sacrificed an opportunity to play a highly significant role in Malayan affairs by its failure to respond to British recognition of the new Chinese regime which would have enable it to set up consulates in Malaya and thus establish a more direct, continuous, and legalized contact with the Chinese community there.

UMNO and MCA joined for the purposes of the municipal elections in Kuala Lumpur and elsewhere in a curious and inevitably unstable alliance which carried the candidates backed by the two groups to a very substantial victory over their upstart rival. It would be pleasant to be able to interpret this move as a victory over communalism but regrettably the evidence indicates that it was rather an effort to safeguard the established and, in one sense or another, privileged communal position of the two parties by joining in a limited agreement to divide the spoils.

Some of the mechanics of this alliance, which have served to overcome the fears of the Chinese for the introduction of the elective principle in Malaya, are exposed in the following analysis by Francis G. Carnell:[16]

"It was at the first Kuala Lumpur municipal elections in February 1952 that the Alliance developed the elections technique which has since carried it to victory elsewhere. By agreement between the local Malay and Chinese leaders, MCA candidates were put up in predominantly Chinese wards and UMNO men in Malay wards. This was the result of an astute recognition of two basic political facts. First, there is in the Malayan plural society a pronounced segregation pattern of Malays and Chinese; the two communities everywhere, whether in town or country-side, tend to live in fairly distinct groups. Secondly, the UMNO-MCA leaders correctly anticipated that in the early days of elections in Malaya, voting is likely to be on a wholly communal basis. All that was needed, therefore, was for the leaders to agree on their respective spheres of influence in Kuala Lumpur. This simple piece of municipal gerrymandering led to a mutually satisfactory sharing of the elected seats between the MCA and UMNO. The Alliance convincingly proved that the praiseworthy belief of the IMP and the Labour Party that, given a non-communal political platform, a Malay can get elected in a Chinese district, or vice versa, is completely utopian under present

[16] *Pacific Affairs*, Sept. 1954, pp. 222–23.

conditions in the Federation. This kind of communal gerrymandering is of course the basis of Ceylon's delimitation of constituencies, but there is no evidence to suggest that the UMNO-MCA leaders were in any way indebted to Ceylon experience."

The demise of the IMP, which had come to be largely Indian in membership, left Dato Onn with no firm political base. Challenging the UMNO-MCA alliance he played a leading role in the organization of the Malayan National Conference of 1953 and from this starting point he established the new Party Negara early in 1954. Although it is predominantly Malay in composition this party put itself forward as an avowedly intercommunal body and will presumably make its largest appeal to moderate and conservative elements. The one other political party of significance is the Pan-Malayan Labour Party, founded in 1952, which explicitly embraces all races and which is seen in some quarters as the hope of the future because of its close relation to the growing trade union movement. Up to the present time, however, none of the Federation's parties, save perhaps the Communists, can claim any very high degree of organization or of penetration into the masses, although the MCA can at least potentially draw upon the different associations which crisscross the Chinese community.

The shortcomings of the present party situation in Malaya found somewhat acidulous but accurate expression in the following comment by a correspondent of *The Times* on the political scene in April 1953:[17]

"There has been a good deal of well-behaved political activity in Malaya recently. . . . In this polite jockeying for position by old friends and acquaintances it is difficult to isolate any salient feature, except that the same notables, middle-class, middle-aged and generally right-wing, are in-

[17] *The Times* (London), April 23, 1953.

volved, and that apart from the UMNO-MCA alliance, no group has a large following. The only other organized group is the Malayan Communist Party."

The role of the government in the communal issue in the Federation has been both difficult and equivocal. Although the official position—as contained, for example, in the directive to General Templer as High Commissioner—is that a united Malayan nation should be achieved which could in due course become fully self-governing, there are informed critics who are prepared to go so far as to read into the government's actions an actual intent to delay Malayan advance through the classical tactics of divide and rule. As has been seen above, the planning carried on in London during the war looked to a redressing of the balance in favor of the Chinese and a rationalization of the anachronistic political structure of the peninsula, but second thoughts under Malay and other pressures brought speedy restoration of the prerogatives of the Sultans and a new strengthening of the Malay hand. Under the Federation Agreement the High Commissioner was charged with the responsibility of safeguarding the special position of the Malays and of protecting the rights, powers, and dignity of the Sultans. That the Malays have a better claim than the peoples of other races to regard Malaya as their homeland and that they deserve special backing and encouragement remain cardinal points in the basic British policy.

On the other hand, very careful attention to the interests and opinions of the Chinese is dictated not only by their numerical and economic strength in the country but also by the fact that, according to the usual estimate, the guerrilla forces are some ninety-five percent Chinese in composition and have received the great bulk of their support from the Chinese community. It is beyond question that that community has in it large numbers of people who are in no way responsive to the Communist appeal even after the success of Communism in China itself, but it is equally beyond question that there are many Chinese who are sitting on the fence waiting to see how events will turn. On the evidence available it is not unreasonable to assume that the bulk of the Chinese community is as yet uncommitted to a final position. It would be absurd to assume that any single answer will emerge to embrace the whole of a community which ranges up and down from millionaires to poverty-stricken coolies, from relatively recent arrivals to old-established Malayan-Chinese families, from hardened Communist guerrilla fighters to staunch reactionaries. But, given the traditional Chinese cohesiveness, it is to be expected that there will gradually emerge a dominant Chinese attitude which will be determined both by what happens in Malaya and by developments in China itself. Certainly it can be said that the Chinese community is not content with its present status in Malaya.

To show further favor to the Malays—which, where financial outlay is involved, is necessarily largely at the cost of the Chinese taxpayer—is to alienate the Chinese whose loyal support must be won for any viable Malayan scheme of things, and to drive more of them toward or into the Communist camp. Similarly, any advance in the political status of the Chinese can only be made at the risk of undermining the loyalty of the Malay community which has begun to be aware of the very real dangers which threaten it. There is, in fact, almost no significant action or decision which the government can take which does not work to the advantage of one of the two communities and which cannot be interpreted as being deliberately prejudicial to the other.

A central bone of contention, which becomes of even greater consequence with the advent of representative institutions, is the question of citizenship for the non-Malay peoples in general and particularly for the Chinese. To attempt to operate a democratic system in a country in which a very large proportion of the most active and enterprising elements of the population, controlling a great part of its economic life, are excluded from citizenship is obviously a highly hazardous enterprise. One of the features of the Malayan Union proposal to which the Malays most objected was that which conferred Malayan citizenship widely on the Chinese and other non-Malays, and the Federation Agreement pulled back sharply in the other direction. A new change of front came in 1952 with the adoption by both the Federation and the States of citizenship legislation which again partially let down the bars to the non-Malays and went some way toward finding an acceptable answer. There is no need to seek to explore here the details of this intricate legislation,[18] but in inadequate summary of some of its major provisions it might be said that it operates to bestow Federal citizenship (1) on citizens of the United Kingdom and its colonies who meet certain Malayan conditions, without impairing their prior nationality, and (2) on others who meet the requirements established for qualifying as a subject of one of the Malay Sultans and hence as a national of one of the nine States. In this second category citizenship is bestowed on anyone born in a Malay State if one of his parents had also been born in the Federation and is open by registration or naturalization to others who have resided in the Federation for specified periods of years, are of good character, speak Malay or English with reasonable proficiency, and take an oath of loyalty to the Federation and of allegiance to the Ruler, renouncing any citizenship or nationality other than that (if they happen to possess it) of the United Kingdom or colonies. It has been estimated that under the new statutes something over one million Chinese would be citizens, or

[18] For an exposition of the legal and political background and intricacies of the citizenship problem, see F. G. Carnell, "Malayan Citizenship Legislation," *International and Comparative Law Quarterly*, Oct. 1952, pp. 504–18.

between fifty and sixty percent of the Federation's Chinese population. In addition some thirty percent of the Indian population became citizens by law with others in a position to qualify by application. Since about ninety-eight percent of the Malaysians have citizenship, it was expected that over seventy percent of the total population of the Federation could now have the status of citizens. The tying of citizenship to State nationality, which was at least in part dictated by considerations of a legal-constitutional order, appeared to many a retrograde step, prolonging a parochialism which had outlived its usefulness and tending to hamper the evolution of a single Malayan nation. Its actual effects in this connection will largely depend on the extent to which the formal status of State nationality comes to be outweighed in importance by the political and other benefits to be derived from Federal citizenship.

The resolution of this long and often bitter controversy, even though in a fashion which wholly satisfied few, was one of the major steps which needed to be taken to clear the way for a Malayan nation, but it would be a mistake to attach too great importance to the formal acquisition of citizenship, particularly in a political entity as peculiar and hybrid as the Federation of Malaya. Although the denial of citizenship may act to bar loyalty, there can be no guarantee that its acquisition will evoke the necessary emotional response of devotion to this nation and the inner foreswearing of the deep ties which lead elsewhere. For nation-building purposes an even more significant issue, which has also received much embattled consideration in the postwar years, is the creation of an educational system which would serve to bring the communities together in language and culture. As Victor Purcell puts it: "The people of Malaya, who are divided into several races, are divided also, and quite as effectively, by the kind of education they happen to receive."[19] One of the most legitimate

[19] "The Crisis in Malayan Education," *Pacific Affairs*, March 1953, p. 70.

grounds for criticism of the British policy in Malaya in the prewar decades was the general meagerness of the educational system and in particular the lack of attention to the Chinese who largely provided their own education in their own fashion under government supervision.

In the postwar period the educational problem has received far more attention than it did before and the school system has been markedly expanded, although there are still many children who are without education. As far as general policy is concerned, surveys undertaken in the Federation to blueprint the proper lines of development for the future have come to contradictory conclusions depending essentially on the pro-Malay or pro-Chinese bias of those conducting them. An official determination has now been made, however, that the desirable goal is a single national school system which would provide a six year course of free primary education with a Malayan orientation for pupils of all races, but it is obvious that there is a vast amount to be accomplished before any such program can be put into full operation. It need scarcely be said that the Chinese are as reluctant to abandon their language and culture as are the Malays (and the British) to see large-scale public support of schools which are Chinese in character. The recent decision of the Chinese to establish a Chinese university in Malaya is a further sign of the difficulties which lie ahead. To plan a national school system with a Malayan orientation is both admirable and necessary, but it will be impossible to put content into the words without seriously tipping the scales of the communal balance to one side or the other.

Recognizing the dangers of both communalism and Communism, the government appears now to have adopted a policy of encouraging the more conservative or moderate elements of the several races in efforts to move toward the formation of a Malayan nation which would not, at least in the early stages, be overly demanding. On this basis it is widely believed that some element of official blessing entered into the founding of the IMP and also into the calling of the National Conference, referred to above, at which the prime ministers of seven of the states met with a number of spokesmen of all races to draw up a plan for a "united, self-governing Malayan nation." It has indeed been suggested that one of the reasons for the relative weakness of the recent moves toward inter-communal cooperation is precisely the suspicion of governmental inspiration which drives away leaders looking toward more drastic and speedy change.

As the situation now stands in Malaya it is still the British who control a colonial system. A start has been made on the Malayanization of the civil service, including the hesitant admission to it of non-Malays, but it is a slow process and has barely begun to reach the higher brackets of the service. If at least the military phase of the Emergency is drawing to a close, both because of the successes of General Templer's policies and because of a change in Communist strategy, it may be that a speedier end will be put to colonialism than seemed likely a short time back, but under present circumstances it is hard to take exception to the harsh comments of Francis G. Carnell:[20]

"The Malayan nation is as yet little more than a polite fiction. It amounts to a Federation flag, the nucleus of an army which the Chinese hesitate to join, a citizenship from which at least forty percent of the Chinese, many of them locally born, are still excluded, and the right of less than ten percent of the population of seven municipalities and towns in the Federation to cast a local government vote. . . . Western democracy is, for the most part, still a meaningless concept in Malaya. There have been few evidences of it in action."

[20] "Communalism and Communism in Malaya," *Pacific Affairs*, June 1953, pp. 113–14. For a later version of his views based in part upon his estimate of the significance and effects of the reforms introduced in 1954, see his article, referred to above, in *Pacific Affairs*, Sept. 1954.

As a result of the recent reforms the seeds of representative institutions have been planted, but they have been given no great encouragement to grow; and the soil in which they must take root is infertile. Since 1948 the stringent Emergency regulations and controls, now somewhat relaxed, have had a markedly restrictive and deadening effect which, in part through the curbs imposed on free association and expression, have delayed developments which might otherwise have taken place. The British are reluctant to take steps which they fear would plunge the country, as the Colonial Secretary, Oliver Lyttelton, put it in mid-1952, "into such racial strife, conflict and confusion as they have not yet seen." The Malays are unprepared to abandon such political power and privilege as they still have, and the Chinese will not enter into the occasionally proposed trade by which they would sacrifice to the Malays a larger share in the country's economy in order to secure a more equal political footing. The proposal is from time to time put forward that the one line of development which will achieve the desired results is the building of a Socialist society. As a correspondent of the *New Statesman and Nation* recently phrased it:[21]

"Economists are convinced that the only possible hope for a Malayan nationalism, and a Malayan nation, is through Socialism, or through some economic policy which will put the two big groups of people, roughly equal in number, the Malays and the Chinese, on a more or less comparable footing."

There is much which is attractive in such a proposal, but it must be recognized that there is no magic in the term "Socialism" which can by itself overcome communal cleavage. Even more in a Socialist than in a free enterprise society the inevitable question is posed as to who has the dominant

[21] "Socialist Malaya," Sept. 12, 1953, p. 280. Much the same position is taken by Derrick Sington in the pamphlet, *Malayan Perspective*, cited above.

and controlling voice, and peace and harmony would emerge only if the two major communities were prepared to merge or collaborate in constructive enterprise, the Malays conceding political equality to the Chinese and the Chinese surrendering economic dominance to a neutral or truly national state.

Beneath the strong framework of the British colonial regime, communalism rather than nationalism still dominates the Malayan scene. In such circumstances only the most optimistic could hope for the successful operation of full-fledged parliamentary institutions; but it may well be that only a bold and imaginative move in that direction by the British can produce the lacking unity. "Unless the people of Malaya are given a chance to crawl in the democratic nursery they can scarcely be expected to stand up in Asia confronting all comers as an adult, independent people."[22]

The extraordinarily difficult and perhaps impossible task of creating a Malayan nation, presumably an indispensable prerequisite for representative government, has hardly been begun. In moving toward it almost every aspect of the country's life and structure must be reconsidered. Even the first necessity of putting an end to Communist terrorism can by no means be dealt with solely on the military level but demands a wide variety of social, economic, and political actions and reforms.[23] Furthermore, although the present division of Malaya into Singapore and a Federation composed of nine States and two Settlements can be seen as something of an advance in rationalization over the prewar structure, the Federation remains an overly complex piece of political machinery for a small country, and

[22] Victor Purcell, "The Chinese in Malaya," *The Times* (London), Dec. 15, 1952. See also his "General Templer," *The Twentieth Century*, Feb. 1954, pp. 118–29.

[23] Some of the key contemporary problems are dealt with by John Kerry King, "Malaya's Resettlement Problem," *Far Eastern Survey*, March 1954, pp. 33–40.

the separation between it and Singapore is obviously an arbitrary one. Any major tinkering with this machinery, however, immediately touches vital nerves of the communal problem. To join Singapore to the Federation is to increase the political strength of the Chinese, and to build up the significance and central powers of the Federation is to weaken the States which continue to be the strongholds of the Malays.

In Malaya, as elsewhere where there is deep-rooted original ethnic diversity, the introduction of representative institutions is certain to raise in even more drastic form than before the question as to which are the communities which are to be represented. The posing of this question in India led to partition, but no such solution is conceivable for Malaya. No consideration of the future of the country can fail to take account of what may prove to be the most fundamental factor of all. As against the potential charms of a still-to-be created Malayan nation, there is the pull of China on the Chinese and of India on the Indians; and an independent Indonesia must have its strong attraction for a Malay people outnumbered in its own country.

CHAPTER FIVE

The Philippines

By Willard H. Elsbree

IF REPRESENTATIVE democracy is to take root anywhere in Southeast Asia, the Philippines would seem to offer the most fertile ground for its development. Culturally, historically, politically, this country has certain advantages in attempting to transplant Western political forms to a quite different environment. Three centuries of Spanish rule produced an upper class whose family and cultural ties with Spain gave it a distinctly Western orientation. The lives of the great majority of the people, however, have been affected only slightly by Western influences. Roman Catholicism, introduced during this same period and adopted by the mass of the population, has been another important Westernizing influence; moreover, its precepts and ideas have not met with the resistance of a strongly organized Oriental religion. The spread of Catholicism brought with it the beginning of Western type education and a system of public schools was introduced as early as 1863. Under American auspices there was a marked expansion in both educational facilities and the number of pupils so that the current rate of literacy is approximately fifty percent. Even taking into account the superficial nature of some of this literacy, this is a figure which compares favorably with that of any other Southeast Asian country. Politically, during American rule, the goal of eventual self-government was accepted at a comparatively early date. Political parties advocating immediate independence were permitted after 1906, and there was a gradual but fairly consistent extension of governmental powers to the Filipinos with the result that the transition to independence was made with relative smoothness.

In spite of these favorable conditions, serious doubt exists about the future of democratic government in the islands. To explore fully the nature of these doubts would involve a detailed political, social, and economic analysis. Some notion of the difficulties, however, can be gained from a consideration of certain problems involving Philippine political institutions, in particular, the executive and its relation with the legislature, political parties, and elections.

Quite naturally, the formal structure of the Philippine government closely follows the American pattern. The men who framed the constitution were influenced by the fact that their product was subject to American approval. Of even more importance, they, and the men who have operated the government, were acquainted most intimately with American political institutions and practices.

The constitutional structure established for the Commonwealth in 1936 has been continued since independence was proclaimed in July 1946. One of the chief differences between the Philippine constitution and its American model is that the former, while maintaining the traditional separation of powers, gives a wider grant of authority to the president who is now chosen by popular vote for a four-year term (and is limited to eight years in office). The legislature is a bicameral one composed of a House of Representatives chosen for a four-year term from electoral districts and a Senate whose members are chosen by a national vote for a six-year term, one-third of the total membership of twenty-four being elected every two years. The judicial system is topped by a Supreme Court with the power of judicial review. The government is centralized, not federal, in form, with many important local officials appointed by the president. Suffrage is extended to men and women who have reached the age of twenty-one with the qualification, important in the Philippines, that they be literate.

An important postwar political development was the break-up of the dominant political party, the Nacionalistas, into two factions, one of which retained the old label and one which was named the Liberal Party. The latter, under the leadership of Manuel Roxas, who had remained in the Philippines during the war, assumed control of the government as the result of the first postwar election in April 1946. The Nacionalistas were led by Sergio Osmena, who had succeeded to the presidency upon the death of Manuel Quezon in the United States where the government moved after the Japanese invasion. After his defeat, Osmena retired from active political life and the next standard-bearer of the Nacionalistas was Jose Laurel, the leader of the administration established by the Japanese Occupation. The significance of this split will be considered later.

While the constitution generally followed the American pattern, a different environment inevitably yielded a quite different product and practice has modified formal structure. This is evident in the office of the Philippine president. Even in origin it was vested with greater power than its American model, in part, because it was felt that the Philippine tradition demanded it, in part, because the period when it was established was one marked by distrust of the competency of legislatures and a demand for executive leadership in almost every Western country. This was reflected in the Philippine constitution by giving the president extensive budgetary powers, by strictly limiting the right of the legislature to increase budget appropriations, by granting the president the right of item veto and sweeping emergency powers, and by giving him broad authority over governmental economic enterprises and over local government.

An enumeration of the formal powers of the president is only a partial measure of the actual authority he enjoys. Tradition and circumstance have added others equally as important. It is a truism that the development of any political office is moulded by the nature of the men who occupy it, and Philippine presidents have been strong figures, not reticent about exercising their authority. Manuel Quezon, the first incumbent, was probably the outstanding personality in modern Philippine history. Not only was he not averse to power, his very prestige meant that power was often thrust upon him even when he did not seek it. His successors may not have enjoyed the national popularity he did, but they have continued to dominate the government. His dramatic action of setting up offices in the Legislative Palace to direct personally the enactment of his initial policies has not become a precedent but executive direction of legislation has. This direction has been so extensive that, in 1949, one prominent Congressman noted that not one of the important bills passed by Congress had originated with one of its members; all were administration-sponsored measures.[1]

The growth of executive leadership has characterized Western democracies, and few would quarrel with the argument that it is essential for a country like the Philippines. The fact remains, however, that it is important to have checks on this leadership at various points in the political structure. The failure of the Philippine government to develop well-defined checks—institutional or otherwise—is a source of danger to the growth of democracy there. The legislature has not had the power, prestige or,

[1] Quintin Paredes, quoted in the *Philippine Free Press*, Jan. 22, 1949.

often, even the will to fill this role adequately[2] and public opinion, predisposed to strong leadership, is a fragile bar in view of the lack of political awareness on the part of the mass of the population. Moreover, the lack of a "constitutional tradition" has made it easy for an administration to push through constitutional changes or even ignore constitutional provisions. Thus, the term of office of the presidency was changed and the president made eligible for re-election even before the first president's term had expired. This was done not as a matter of principle but to make possible President Quezon's re-election. Later, President Roxas reduced the membership of the Supreme Court to seven, in spite of the constitutional provision that it should consist of eleven members. Full membership has now been restored, however.

The equivocal position of Congress was illustrated in a recent dispute with the president over the latter's emergency powers. The constitutional provision giving the president the power to "promulgate rules and regulations to carry out declared national policy" during an emergency was put into effect during the war. In 1952, Congress repealed the grant of these powers but was met by a prompt presidential veto which it was not able to override. The persuasiveness of Congressional protests that the president was prolonging the emergency for his own purposes was vitiated by the action of several Congressmen, some of whom had voted for repeal, who petitioned the president to use these powers to enact a public works measure providing funds for local projects of interest to them. Control over such funds, commonly referred to as the "pork barrel," is a trump card in the hand of the president who can, and does, use it effectively to force legislative compliance.

On the question of emergency powers, however, the

[2] One should except, of course, the recent Senate which was controlled by the opposition and which had the will, if not the power, to impose checks on the executive.

Supreme Court came to the aid of Congress in an important decision late in 1953.[3] In this decision, the Court upheld the repeal of the grant of emergency powers on the grounds that such a grant was intended only for a limited period and that Congress alone was to decide the existence of an emergency. Even at the risk of slow action, said the Court, democratic procedures "must be preferred to concentration of powers in any one man or group of men." In this and another decision mentioned below rendered in the same year, the Supreme Court placed limitations on the actions of the president and displayed an attitude which, if continued, would make it a vital institution in the structure of government.

In the United States, there has been a striking increase in the use of legislative powers of investigation as a check on the actions and policies of the executive branch. The Philippine Congress has undertaken such investigations but they have yet to become an effective instrument of control. In 1950, an investigative committee was set up by the Senate to examine the whole field of government finance, particularly the activities of the governmental corporations against which there were widespread charges of corruption. When the opposition party captured control of the Senate the following year, the committee inevitably became a part of the political quarrel between that body and the president, but it filled a useful function as a sounding board of grievances against the administration. One is forced to the conclusion, however, that without presidential cooperation, or at least neutrality, the accomplishments of any congressional investigation must be limited. Several officials were ordered by the president not to appear before the committee and some were given protection when an attempt was made to arrest them. Moreover, the attitude of Congressmen toward previous investigations indicated

[3] Senate President Eulogio Rodriguez *et al* v. National Treasurer Vincente Gella *et al*.

something less than full-hearted devotion to their use as a matter of principle.[4]

Among the reasons why Congress has not developed into a more effective buffer against executive power, two might be cited, its failure to acquire prestige and almost continuous one party government. The corruption scandals which have plagued the government since the end of the war have implicated several Congressmen with the result that those interested in "cleaning up the mess" have not regarded Congress as a useful instrument of reform. Then, too, the general conduct of its business has not inspired public confidence. Hayden's description of conditions at the end of sessions of the National Assembly apply to the present as well.[5] A high percentage of bills are passed amid the confusion surrounding the legislative logjam at the end when it is often impossible to determine which bills have been passed, whether they have been passed or in what form. Legally established procedures are widely disregarded, a practice which frequently makes it easier for the administration to push through its measures.

These conditions are by no means unique to the Philippines; a student of American state legislatures would find much that is familiar. Elsewhere, however, the damage is partially mitigated by the work of committees which have given measures previous consideration. In the Philippine legislature, committees have not assumed so much power and importance. Hayden's criticisms of them, the large number in proportion to total membership, the lack of

[4] See the report of a Liberal Party caucus in the *Philippine Free Press*, Jan. 22, 1949. At this meeting, Senator Jose Avelino reportedly attacked the administration for undertaking investigations which, he held, were hurting the party. Abuses by the party in power should be tolerated, he is supposed to have said. President Quirino reportedly favored the investigations on the grounds that public opinion demanded them and that the party would gain prestige.

[5] Hayden, Joseph R., *The Philippines: A Study in National Development*, New York, 1942, pp. 188–89.

specialization due to rapid turnover of membership and of chairmen, the brief consideration given most bills, appear to be as true today as when they were written.[6]

Low standards of performance on the part of legislatures have damaged the cause of representative democracy in the West, witness the example of France. They could be even more injurious, if not fatal, in the Philippines where democracy is just struggling to get on its feet.

Executive control over the legislature has been reinforced by one party domination of the government. Since presidents have been the actual, if not titular, party leaders, executive policies have been party policies as well. Consequently the legislature has been less prone to exert its independence than would be the case if there were periods of opposition control or even if there were a well-established opposition party. Differences of opinion have been reflected in intra-party struggles rather than in executive-legislative contests.

If both the Liberals and the Nacionalistas should maintain their present strength, an important turning point in Philippine politics may have been reached. A better balance between executive and legislative power might be achieved, and the competition for popular support might produce significant changes in governmental policies with more attention paid to interests now of minor influence. This may well prove to be the case, but it is too early to make any firm prediction. It is quite conceivable that the sweeping victory of the Nacionalistas in the national election of 1953 will usher in a new period of one party domination.

Although one party government has served to place the legislature in a minor role, it would not be fatal, necessarily, to representative government. Presidential powers might be checked by other party personalities and factions; interest groups might still find expression within the party.

[6] Hayden, *op. cit.*, pp. 178 ff.

Unquestionably, however, one party government enhances the position of the president, thanks to his role as party leader and dispenser of party patronage which includes at times the distribution of party nominations. It also raises the question: how representative are Philippine political parties?

It would not be unfair to characterize parties in the Philippines as coalitions of personal factions and local political bosses. These groups were brought together and maintained within one party, the Nacionalista, largely as a result of the struggle for independence which united all politically conscious Filipinos. Because of its near-monopoly of the government, the party was able to build up a machine and to attract to itself the best political talent of the country. Other parties, for the most part, have been the outgrowth of factional quarrels within the Nacionalistas or the struggle for leadership, such as that between Quezon and Sergio Osmena. The leaders of the Young Philippines Party were interested in opposition for its own sake for they felt it essential to democratic government. A similar view motivated many of the political activities of Mr. Juan Sumulong. Unity in the demand for independence and the fact that the Nacionalistas offered the best avenue for political success, however, generally brought other groups back into the Nacionalista fold.

The present two party alignment resulted from a postwar split within the party which was mentioned earlier. At first glance, it might appear to mean that, with independence achieved, divisive questions were taking precedence in Philippine politics. Party programs do not bear this out. Slight differences in emphasis, the question of ratification of the Japanese peace treaty, for example, represent convenient political weapons rather than any basic cleavage in policy. Significantly, the chief and most effective issue of the opposition has been graft and corruption in the administration.

Representative government does not require parties to espouse distinct and divergent principles; on the contrary, agreement on basic objectives is necessary for it to function at all. Of greater significance are the questions whether or not economic and social interest groups find representation within the parties and whether the parties can successfully compromise differences among them.

Viewed from this standpoint, Philippine parties are found to have serious shortcomings. Both parties and the government have been dominated by a homogeneous group which is, socially, the product of Western influence and which, economically, reflects the interests of a wealthy commercial and large landowning class. Can it successfully represent the interests of the mass of the population untouched, or only superficially so, by Westernization and with far different economic demands? Undoubtedly, the ruling group enjoyed popular support in the fight for independence, but can this unity continue in the face of many problems which must be met now?

Reform of land ownership and control is an acute issue. Tenancy is widespread and has been increasing at the same time that incomes of large landowners have been rising. Conditions surrounding tenancy are appalling in some areas and there has been little improvement. According to the Bell Mission Report: "The strained relationship between landlords and their tenants and the low economic condition generally of the tillers of the soil compose one of the main factors retarding the recovery of agricultural production."[7] Redistribution of land, reduction of rent, improved credit facilities may not solve the basic agricultural problems of increased productivity and a wider diversification of crops but they are crucial political issues because a large part of the population sees its relief in these forms.

[7] *Report to the President of the United States by the Economic Survey Mission to the Philippines,* Washington, D.C.: Government Printing Office, Oct. 9, 1950, p. 55.

Can a government enact and, equally important, enforce reforms which strike at the privileges of a group on which that government leans so heavily for support? There is a law on the statute books reserving seventy percent of the crop yield to the tenant farmer but it is honored as much in the breach as in the observance. If demand for agrarian reform cannot find expression in a political party and achieve at least its minimum demands by the regular processes of government, it inevitably will assume violent forms.

This is an aspect of the Hukbalahap rebellion which must not be overlooked. The Huks, organized to wage guerrilla warfare against the Japanese, have operated in several areas but their chief source of strength has been Central Luzon, where the rate of tenancy is extremely high and the conditions of the peasantry among the worst in the Philippines. The leadership of the movement has been in Communist hands but the ranks have been filled by the discontented peasantry driven to resort to force as the only apparent means of improving its lot. In the late 1940's the Huks gained control over several areas and a full-scale civil war seemed possible. An aggressive anti-Huk campaign, directed by Ramon Magsaysay, the Secretary of Defense from 1950 until 1953, has driven them from many of their positions and has badly crippled the movement by breaking up the nerve center of its operations in Manila.

Part of the campaign has been to sponsor resettlement projects for captured and surrendered Huks such as the one in Mindanao, an island where there are large areas of unused land. The government thus has recognized the connection between the rebellion and the need for land reform. Such projects are, of course, costly, and the limited financial resources of the government severely hamper its program. Resettlement, moreover, is only a partial solution and, to date, the government has failed to produce a policy to deal with the problem more comprehensively. The military threat of the rebellion has receded but the economic and social forces which lay behind it remain.

With the bulk of the agrarian population politically inarticulate (much of it is disfranchised by the literacy requirement for voting) and with the government closely allied with a group tied to the status quo, whence is to come the impetus for change? If there were a strong, native middle class, whether professional, commercial, or composed of small, independent landowners, a government based on its support could carry through a reform program. Such a class has failed to develop extensively in the Philippines and the lack of it raises some doubt about the future of democracy there. Whether or not a middle class is essential to democracy remains a moot question but the close connection that has existed between the two furnishes some justification for this doubt.

The role of a commercial middle class has been filled partly by the Chinese, who are important in the retail trade and as money lenders. The Chinese population is now over 250,000 but anti-Chinese sentiment has kept them from playing an important role in politics. Their main participation is in the form of "voluntary contributions" which are the chief source of revenue for the political parties. Anti-Chinese measures are always popular so that the party in power is in an ideal position to exact "squeeze." On the other hand, it is always expedient for the Chinese to maintain good relations with the opposition as well in the event that it should become the majority. The small size and the vulnerability of the Chinese population make it unlikely that they would ever challenge the government openly unless in conjunction with an attack from the outside. In their present unassimilated position, however, they remain a source of political corruption and of potential disaffection.

Urban labor is another section of the population not adequately represented in politics. In the postwar inflation, wages have lagged behind rising prices and real wages did not reach even their prewar level until 1949. (Real wages for agricultural labor have remained below that level.) The result has been, as the Bell Report noted, that real income has been transferred from labor and other low-income groups to the wealthier classes.[8] Low wages, continued unemployment, the lack of strong, independent trade unions have deprived labor of the economic means to improve its condition. A minimum-wage law enacted in 1951 was the result of American, not local, pressure and the government has lacked the resources to give it anything like adequate enforcement. Here, again, the lack of a large middle class is keenly felt. Economically and politically frustrated, labor is another group with few ties to the present order, a fertile field for the activities of anti-democratic forces.

Lack of representativeness is not the only weakness of Philippine parties. Party control rests with a fairly small oligarchy of top party leaders allied with local political bosses and officials. A recent example of the procedure followed in nominating Senatorial candidates is illuminating.

In the 1951 elections, Nacionalista candidates were named by the national directorate of the party, the chief dispute being over the geographical distribution of the nominees. The Liberal Party held a convention at which the delegates staged a fight for the privilege of naming the candidates. The party's executive committee demurred, but finally agreed to allow the convention to choose twenty-four possible nominees from which the committee would select nine names. (Nine seats were at stake in this election.) The final list of Liberal candidates, however, contained four names not among the original twenty-four. These were men added at the insistence of President Quirino, another indication of the power of the

[8] *Ibid.*, pp. 16–17.

president within the party and consequently, over the government.

Representative government assumes fair and honest elections. It cannot begin to function unless eligible voters are free to go to the polls and vote as they please and unless all votes are counted and counted as cast. This basic requirement is not yet firmly established in the Philippines, although the elections of 1951 and 1953 were a vast improvement over that of 1949.

It would tax the ingenuity of the most corrupt political machine in this country to match the practices adopted by the government party in the 1949 election. Registration lists were padded to almost comic proportions; in some districts the number of votes reported equalled the total population. Secrecy of the ballot was widely violated; some polling places were moved at the last minute so that voters could not find them; in at least one instance, voting was stopped as soon as all government supporters had voted. These were only a few of the more refined techniques. Force and intimidation were widespread, particularly in rural areas. The following report by a provincial official is typical: "The election in my province was a sham. . . . Three jeepneys [jeeps converted into small buses] full of gangsters and criminals armed with rifles and sub-machine guns went around the different precincts throughout the province on election day and intimidated Nacionalista and Avelino supporters."[9] The Commission on Elections, established to supervise the conduct of elections and empowered to investigate and correct fraudulent electoral practices, was powerless in the face of the situation. One commissioner charged cabinet officials with deliberate obstruction of the Commission's work and another was led to remark that "there is no more democracy in the Philippines."[10]

[9] Quoted in the *Philippine Free Press*, Nov. 19, 1949.
[10] *Ibid.*, Oct. 29, 1949.

Conditions were far different in 1951, thanks partly to the increased effectiveness of the work of the Commission, partly to the role played by an independent citizens group, the National Movement for Free Elections (known as NAMFREL), but particularly to the activities of the Secretary of National Defense, Ramon Magsaysay. The success of their efforts, however, resulted more from current circumstances than from any basic political change.

The Commission on Elections carried out a wide-scale revision of registration rolls and investigated a far higher percentage of the charges brought before it than previously. In province after province, registration figures were generally reduced, in one instance by as much as fifty percent. How much of the Commission's effectiveness, however, was due to the fact that here it had the support of a president favorably disposed to a clean election? True, on one issue it challenged him and won, but the story of the case offers little encouragement to the cause of free elections.[11] Appointed by the president, with no enforcement powers of its own, the Commission can be stymied at every turn by an administration determined to maintain itself in office.

The force and intimidation which accompanied the 1949 election were checked in most areas in 1951 by Army troops and the ROTC under the direction of Magsaysay. The Constabulary was merged with the Army so that it was no longer at the disposal of provincial governors who often used it for political purposes. Private police forces in the employ of local political leaders, estate and mill owners, and associated with some of the more flagrant abuses in previous elections, were held in check. Here, again,

[11] The Commission annulled fraudulent registration in one precinct in Cavite and ordered a completely new registration. The President disputed its power to do this but accepted the decision of the Supreme Court supporting the Commission. He proceeded, however, to remove from office the mayor of Cavite who was the leader of the faction which brought the charges before the Commission.

presidential acquiescence was vital to success. Cabinet members serve at the discretion of the executive and their powers of office are readily transferable. Army officials, backed by the administration, could checkmate any Defense Secretary. The Army is, after all, a flexible instrument which could be used by the regime to maintain itself in power as well as to ensure fair elections.

The National Movement for Free Elections is a nonpartisan organization devoting its efforts to the political education of the public and to the cause of honest elections. It symbolizes the type of role which a strong middle class could play in Philippine politics and its weaknesses reflect the weaknesses of that class. Its chief support comes from business and professional groups in the larger urban centers; at the barrio level it is, at most, only a name. Significantly, it is largely an American-inspired organization, American-financed and equipped with American-prepared literature. Without a firm base in the local population, it would scarcely be able to withstand pressures brought against it by a determined opposition.

The hopeful indications of 1951 were continued in the 1953 election. This is particularly significant because the presidency and, hence, the whole administration was at stake. Prior to the election, there were many predictions that the Liberals, with President Quirino again at the head of the ticket, would resort to the tactics of 1949 to insure their hold on the government. The candidate of the Nacionalistas was Ramon Magsaysay, who quit the cabinet and the Liberals early in 1953 and whose leadership in the anti-Huk campaign had brought him national prominence.

Throughout the bitterly fought campaign there were rumors of impending fraud and violence: that ink eradicator was being sent to polling places to change ballots, that officials and teachers favorable to the Nacionalistas had been removed from their positions. Nacionalista rallies were broken up in some areas and the removal of the Constabulary from the Army aroused fears that it would again be used to terrorize the voters.

The result of the election was an overwhelming victory for Magsaysay and the Nacionalista Party which gained a heavy majority in both houses of the legislature. The dire forebodings of wide-scale fraud were not borne out. There were sporadic instances of violence, a few deaths, and the resort to terrorism in some spots,[12] but these resulted from local conditions rather than any concerted government campaign. There was no partisan intervention by the armed forces and the work of the Commission on Elections was carried on before and during the election without interference.[13]

Among the factors influencing the conduct of the election, two might be mentioned. The government was aware that the campaign was being closely watched by the outside world. The United States, while bending over backward to preserve a neutral attitude toward the two parties, made it quite clear that its greatest interest was in a free election. A government elected by grossly fraudulent means would be in a poor position to request badly needed economic and military aid. Secondly, the insistence of the opposition on a free election and its organization to insure it meant that the government, if it resorted to strong-arm methods, would be faced with the danger of virtual civil war. In a sense, the chief issue in the campaign was that of free elections, and the cause won an important battle, though, perhaps, not yet the war.

The election brought to the presidency a new type in Philippine politics. Magsaysay, the son of a farmer, represents a social background widely different from that of

[12] See *New York Times* report, Nov. 11, 1953. For a more extensive examination of the election of 1953, see Willard H. Elsbree, "The 1953 Philippine Presidential Elections," *Pacific Affairs,* March 1954, pp. 3–15.

[13] One of the commissioners declared that the election was the best conducted one since the war. *Ibid.,* Nov. 12, 1953.

past Filipino political leaders, and his career and reputation have not been built in politics. Many of the men around him come from middle-class professional and business circles. Not career politicians, they have entered politics in the interest of change and reform. The chief weapon in the hands of Magsaysay and his supporters was the charge of corruption in the administration and they successfully capitalized on the widespread "it's-time-for-a-change," "throw-the-rascals-out" feeling. They have won a victory but it is by no means complete or final. Will they be able to translate it into an operative program? Will Magsaysay be able to effect real, not merely paper, reforms? Will the reformist element become the captive of the Nacionalista "old guard," representative of the traditionally dominant class in Philippine politics? The answers to questions such as these will largely determine the future course of representative democracy in the Philippines.

The development of local self-government in the Philippines was one of the first objectives of the American regime. It sought to build a foundation for democracy on a national scale by replacing the centralized form of administration, which had characterized Spanish rule, by one which allowed greater local autonomy and which would be run by Filipinos.

The Filipinization of local government was readily achieved, but decentralization of authority has proven to be more difficult. If anything, independence had increased the pressures for greater central control and has expanded the area of operations of the national government at the local level. This is due partly to the influence of past experience—after all, even the American program to broaden local autonomy was one which came from the top down. Independence tends to foster centralization for there is less resistance to an administration considered one's own than to one controlled by a foreign power. More important, however, has been the feeling that central control is necessary to maintain minimum standards of government and to introduce new programs. The weight of custom and tradition is felt most strongly at the local level. There has been a sense of urgency, on the part of the national leaders, for modernization, improvement, increased efficiency. The impetus for change, they have felt, must come from the top; to wait for it to be generated at the local level would create an intolerable delay.

The two main divisions of Philippine local government are the provinces, which generally follow traditional boundaries and which are classified according to revenue, and the municipalities, which consist of a headquarters town and the surrounding villages and rural area. The popular election of provincial and municipal councils and executives, the governor and mayor respectively, has not served to check the trend toward centralization. This trend is signified by the growth, particularly after World War II, of the number of chartered cities which are even more closely under the supervision of the central government. In these cities, the mayor, vice-mayor, and sometimes even council members are appointed by the president.

Although the creation of chartered cities has not loosened central control, it has sought to free the larger cities from the close supervision by provincial authorities which characterizes Philippine local government. It could be said that the chief function of the provincial government is supervision of the municipalities, particularly in the fields of finance and policing.

Even elected mayors are subject to presidential authority for both President Quezon and Quirino used their power to suspend mayors from office. A recent decision of the Supreme Court, however, would seem to limit the president's authority in this matter.[14] In this case, President Quirino suspended the mayor of Manila, an elective

[14] Mayor Arsenio Lacson v. Acting Mayor Bartolome Gatmaitan *et al.*

official, on the grounds of "moral turpitude." The mayor, Arsenio Lacson, had been indicted for libel on the basis of his remarks about the decision of a Manila judge whom he referred to as "stupid." The court nullified the president's action which, it declared, had not been in accordance with due process of law. The mere filing of information against an official was held not to constitute sufficient grounds for removal which, the court said, could only be for just cause and under due process.

The provincial governments have a very limited autonomy vis-à-vis the national government. This is illustrated most clearly in matters of finance where all key personnel are presidential appointees. These include the provincial treasurer who is responsible for tax collection (the municipal treasurer is also appointed by the president), the auditor, who assesses real property, and the members of the Board of Tax Appeals.

The range of local government is delimited further by the authority of the national representatives who operate at the local level. Health, education, public works, for example, are under the jurisdiction of the national government, primarily, and officials in these fields are responsible to their respective departments in the national government. The high degree of centralization in education is illustrative. The chain of command runs directly from the Secretary of Education to the Director of Public Schools, to the superintendents and, ultimately, to the classroom teacher. The Director of Public Schools, who supervises the public school system and who is a presidential appointee, exercises very broad powers over curricula, salaries, appointments, school construction, to give only a partial list of the subjects under his jurisdiction. Moreover, the Secretary of Education has a large measure of authority over private schools and colleges to insure their compliance with minimum requirements for courses, facilities, and teacher qualifications.

This degree of centralization in education has been attacked frequently as unduly cumbersome and injurious to initiative, but in the words of a Philippine study of the system, ". . . the business of decentralizing school administration seems to have been subordinated to the more compelling problem of school finance."[15] The fact that only the national government has sufficient financial resources (inadequate as even these may be in terms of total need) to undertake any large-scale programs in such fields is another powerful factor in centralization.

The problem of local government is, in part, the problem of attracting interested and competent personnel. This is not to say that there is a lack of popular interest in the affairs of local government, for it is relatively high, but it is true that the educated, most politically conscious group tends to gravitate toward the national government. Because of the lack of authority to be exercised at the local level and because of the prevailing attitude that effective action must be national, those interested in reform and political action concentrate their efforts on national rather than local affairs. This is part of a larger problem noted elsewhere in this study. In the Philippines, as in the other areas, there appears to be a noticeable drift of the educated, the "bright young men," from the small towns and rural areas to the larger urban centers. This is understandable in view of their personal ambitions and their desire to "do something" for their country, but it makes more difficult a solution of the problems of bridging the gap between the educated group and the rest of the population, and of making representative government a reality at the village level.

The 1953 elections marked the end of the Liberal era in Philippine politics. The opposition, a coalition of Nacionalistas and dissident Liberals who had formed the Democratic Party under the leadership of Carlos Romulo, won

[15] Isidro, A., Canave, J. C., Manalang, P. S., Valdes, M. M., *Compulsory Education in the Philippines*, UNESCO, Paris, 1952, p. 32.

a sweeping victory. A few statistics graphically illustrate its extent. Running against the Liberal incumbent, President Quirino, Ramon Magsaysay, the coalition candidate, polled 2,912,992 votes to his opponent's 1,313,991. He carried all but three of the twenty-eight cities; in Manila alone his majority was nearly 140,000. Of the fifty-two provinces, Quirino carried only four, all of which were in the Ilocano area of northwestern Luzon which was his home territory. The coalition prepared a common slate of candidates for the congressional races and these fared nearly as well. All eight of the Senatorial posts were won by coalition members, thus leaving only three men with the Liberal label in that body. In the elections for the House of Representatives, coalition candidates won sixty-seven, the Liberals thirty-four, with one seat won by an independent.

The main issue in the campaign was whether the election itself would be an honest one. The widespread dissatisfaction with the Liberal regime coupled with Magsaysay's personal popularity made it evident early in the campaign that a fair election would produce an opposition victory. Would the Liberals attempt to retain power by use of the methods employed in 1949? There were indications that such might be the case, the use of "goon squads" to intimidate opposition supporters, registration frauds, pressure on the Army to transfer provincial Constabulary commanders, but counter-action proved to be effective. The Commission on Elections vigorously carried out its functions without interference by the administration. NAMFREL continued its work in the education of the electorate and the detection of fraud. Magsaysay supporters organized to counter any government attempts at intimidation and to police the polls. The Army leadership stood up under the pressure exerted on it and did an effective job in supervising the polling. The authority of the Catholic Church was thrown behind an honest election.

In the face of this mobilization of national opinion, any attempt by the administration to "steal" the election would have invited a virtual civil war. The result was that the election was the cleanest in the Philippines since the end of the war and an important victory for the cause of representative government there.

Honest elections are, of course, only a part of the battle. Of equal, if not greater importance, will be the ability of Magsaysay to translate his reform program into action and the effect of the election on the dominant political forces in the country. Magsaysay's first objective of cleansing the government of corrupt and dishonest officials and of rehabilitating the sad state of some of the government corporations should be realized to a large extent. Honesty and efficiency in government are not basic remedies for the problems facing the Philippines but they can help to restore confidence in the government and counteract a cynicism that could be fatal if too prolonged.

The surrender of the Huk leader, Luis Taruc, in May 1954 shows how effectively the back of that rebellion has been broken. To the extent, however, that the rebellion reflected deep-seated agricultural problems, much remains to be done. Magsaysay's multilateral approach to the land question, stricter enforcement of rent and interest rate controls, land resettlement, improved credit facilities, is a promising one. Will the government be able to finance, (at least in part) these and other reform programs by a revised tax system that effects all groups with greater fairness? Will presently privileged interests accede to higher taxes and stricter enforcement measures? Will the government be able to effect the diversification of the economy it seeks, the attraction of capital to new enterprises, the diversion of capital resources from land to industrial use?

To carry this program into effect, the president obviously will need powerful political support. From what groups backing him may it be expected? The general desire for change and Magsaysay's personal popularity produced a large majority but one too heterogeneous to indicate clearly what it wanted. He was, first of all, the candidate of the Nacionalistas and doubtless could have won without the coalition. The party is now firmly in control of Congress and has vastly strengthened its organization throughout the country. Any effective program must have the backing of influential elements in the party and it is not at all certain that they will be willing to accept extensive social and economic reform. The campaign brought about no change in the party leadership. The old guard is still in control and there has been as yet no indication of any serious challenge to their position from within the party. The relationship which develops between Magsaysay and Nacionalista leaders will determine, in good part, the course of his administration.

The first rift was not long in making an appearance. The immediate issue concerned foreign policy and was raised by a member of the Foreign Office who revived the slogan, "Asia for the Asians." While the speech advanced no specific measures, it had distinctly anti-American overtones and was generally regarded as a challenge to the President's pro-American position. Hasty conferences among party leaders produced conciliatory statements and a disavowal of any intent of shifting the Philippine alignment with the United States. Magsaysay wielded his authority and choked off an open revolt. He has since clearly reiterated his policy of a close tie with the United States and specifically rejected a course of neutrality such as that which India has sought to pursue. To date, his pronouncement has gone without open challenge even though the continuing problem of Philippine economic relations with the United States is a source of ammunition for critics.

The most important significance of the incident, however, did not concern foreign policy, the basic direction of which seems fairly well established; the difference between the "pro-American" and "anti-American" groups is more one of degree than of kind. It was an indication of a struggle for power within the party and of an attempt by a faction of the old guard to assert its leadership. The Foreign Office spokesman was a protege of Claro Recto, veteran Nacionalista leader, who has not been completely happy about Magsaysay's pre-eminent position. While this attempt to undermine Magsaysay's prestige was unsuccessful, it was clearly only the opening skirmish of a battle to determine control of the party.

Prominent among Magsaysay's supporters were members of the younger business and professional groups of which the junior chambers of commerce and NAMFREL leaders would be good examples. As was pointed out previously, they represent a new type in Philippine politics and come from a different background than traditional political leaders. Magsaysay himself might be said to belong to this group as do several of his advisers. It is a group which takes its public duties seriously and is impressed with the need for major reform. However, it lacks both numbers and coherent organizational strength, reflecting in this the continued weakness of the middle class. It can provide leadership but its power is still limited.

The size of Magsaysay's majority in the provinces proved the effectiveness of his appeal to the barrio population. His intensive campaign in the villages set a new record for territory covered and there was an enthusiastic response to him personally and to his promises of improved living conditions in the barrios. Potentially, among the most important results of the election were the increased political interest shown by this group and the fact that the government is now headed by one whom they regard as "their man." This helps to bridge the gap between them and the government but, at the same time, will make more serious their disillusionment if their desires are unfulfilled. As a political force, their influence is limited by the inchoateness of their political expression. They still lack effective organization for the representation of their interests in the government.

One other aspect of the election should be noted, the recurring tendency toward one party supremacy. The Liberal organization is all but shattered; many of its leaders were defeated at the polls and have been indulging in mutual recriminations concerning the responsibility for defeat. The general disfavor into which the party has fallen would seem to indicate that even the remaining Liberal governors and mayors will not survive beyond their present terms, or will do so only by switching party allegiance. (Such a move has been made already by some former Liberal politicians.) In view of its present unpopularity it would not be surprising if the "Liberal" label disappeared, with remnants of the organization, perhaps, forming the nucleus of a new party.

The future of the new Democratic Party, led by Mr. Romulo, is problematical. Its direction comes mainly from ex-Liberal leaders who were dissatisfied with the party command, and it still lacks a firm organizational basis. It was the distinctly junior member of the coalition and after the election, elements in both parties urged a complete merger in the interest of national unity, a familiar pattern in Philippine politics. Both Romulo and top Nacionalista leaders have been hesitant, however. At present, the Democrats are in a good position to profit from possible divisions within the Nacionalista Party and from the dissatisfaction which may arise over its program.

The persistence of one party domination, in large part, is due to the fact that parties remain based primarily on personalities. This will continue to be the case while major groups in the country lack political articulateness and organization. The election showed that there are forces working for a change in this respect but gave no clear indication of the form such a change might take.

CHAPTER SIX

Rural and Urban Self-Government in Southeast Asia

By Virginia Thompson

LOCAL SELF-GOVERNMENT in Southeast Asia, as it developed during the seventy-five years that preceded World War II, has generally been regarded as a failure. Nationalists of the area claim that the imperial powers which governed all the countries of the region except one never had any intention of fostering grass-roots democracy, yet independent Thailand was no more successful than the colonies. Everywhere, either inadvertently or otherwise, contact with the West undermined and largely destroyed existing institutions at the village, town, and provincial levels, and, where these occurred only in embryonic form, almost wholly new administrative units were created. Western forms served as the model for these transformations or creations, although the conditions under which local government had evolved in Europe were not duplicated in Southeast Asia. In time the weakness of the new structures became self-evident, and belated efforts were made to revitalize the traditional local government institutions. But Humpty Dumpty could not be put together again, for the economic and social revolutions which the Southeast Asian peoples had undergone in the interval had made the old order hopelessly anachronistic.

None of the new national states of the area has made a real effort to revive the past—in fact, each has kept largely intact the structure it inherited and some of the principles on which it was based. All of the region's governments, however, have recognized the desirability of a greater measure of local autonomy and in some cases they have set up the machinery for a delegation of powers. Nevertheless the prewar trend towards centralization has persisted, largely because of practical considerations but also because the central authorities cannot decide how far and on what terms they will share their power.

Widespread insecurity and even armed revolt in rural areas, traditions of authority and paternalism, the illiteracy and passivity of the population, the lack of trained cadres, financial stringency, fear of regional separatism and of political rivals—all have combined to perpetuate the status quo and the hoarding of power by those already possessing it. In theory, local government bodies are junior partners of the central authority, inasmuch as they share in the responsibility and cost of government. In practice, however, they have been regarded almost wholly as agents for executing policies formulated by an ever more centralized government which has ensured their docility by keeping them in a state of chronic financial dependence. In every case the changes made in the structure and powers of local government bodies have been imposed from above and have not emanated from nor embodied the expressed desires of the people who are expected to make the system work. Complaints of the abuse of power by local officials or councillors on the part of the people under their administration have not been wanting, and there have been periodic requests for larger financial allocations. But the demonstrated ability to use, wisely and conscientiously, such authority as local bodies possess has not been such as to inspire the central government to press more powers upon them. And, most essential of all, there seems to be no genuine popular demand for any greater local autonomy that would entail heavier responsibilities.

In pre-colonial days, the theoretically absolute power of Southeast Asian rulers was diluted by the practical impossibility of imposing their authority in outlying areas. The absence of transportation facilities and of a strong national army and police left effective fiscal and magisterial power largely in the hands of hereditary or locally chosen provincial personalities. So long as the latter provided the central government with sufficient taxes and conscripts, they were left largely undisturbed in the exercise of powers that were undivided, often overlapping, and sometimes contradictory. This confusion of authority seems to have been congenial, or at least acceptable, to the Southeast Asian mind. But the Western nations, as they came to control the region, found it perplexing, impractical for purposes of efficient administration, and offensive to their political concepts. The tempo and extent of the transformation which the colonial powers and Thailand effected in the region's local government institutions differed with the individual country, but the net result everywhere was much the same.

Burma and Vietnam, which became colonies through military conquest, were transformed more rapidly and more completely than were Indonesia and the Straits Settlements (governed as part of India until 1867), which came under Western control gradually by way of trading companies that were primarily concerned with profits and only reluctantly assumed political control. The British in Burma and the French in Vietnam had first of all to establish and maintain order in countries of which they had neither previous experience nor knowledge. The flight of native mandarins from Cochinchina and the concurrent disappearance of their records forced the conquering French naval officers to improvise an administration as best they could. In Burma, the British, bewildered by the inconsistencies and amorphous nature of existing local institutions, were guided by their experience in India, which unfortunately was irrelevant. In both cases, ignorance and urgency, not willful destructiveness, dictated the courses of action, and inevitably the conquerors seized upon such instruments as came to hand and were recognizably useful to them. Thus, during this period, interpreters and foreign intermediaries often displaced recalcitrant or unadaptable local authorities, and a barrier thus arose between the mass of the populations and their new Western masters.

In Indonesia and the Unfederated Malay States, the Dutch and British governments adopted a policy of indirect rule, and consequently native institutions survived longer in those areas. But even there, the same destructive forces were at work. And Thailand, threatened with the loss of more outlying territory to Britain and France, took steps in 1892 to reorganize its local administration in order to bring frontier areas under more effective control by the central government. After the annexation of Upper Burma, the British in 1886 made mistaken efforts to strengthen the powers of village headmen at the expense of other, equally authentic, local authorities; what had formerly been merely a social and residential agglomeration now became an administrative unit. In Java, the Village Act of 1906, designed to achieve the same objective and also to promote villagers' welfare, transformed that unit into a petty municipality along Western lines. When French civil administration succeeded the government of the admirals in Cochinchina, the principle of the separation of powers was applied there far more thoroughly than by the less theory-ridden British in Burma. The result was an enormous and expensive increase in French officialdom and so great a loss of authority and prestige for the native Notables that many refused to continue in that capacity.

Throughout Southeast Asia, as time went on, existing institutions were progressively undermined by standardization of administrative units, demarcation of their geographical boundaries, delegation of specific duties and clear-cut responsibilities to local officials and governing bodies, and separation of judicial from executive powers. The transformation of outstanding local leaders into minor officials of the central government and the elevation of non-indigenous and transferable individuals to posts of authority made for a more orderly administration and efficient collection of taxes, but it largely destroyed indigenous democracy as it had existed in Southeast Asia's countryside. However, the democratic nature of the area's local government institutions, before their contact with the West, should not be exaggerated, for the role played by the hereditary and propertied elite in rural life was paramount. The superiority of pre-colonial village leadership derived from the sanction given by custom, concentration of powers, permanency, and knowledge based on long local experience. The new officials were often alien to the area administered, frequently rotated in posts, and almost always impinged upon the authority of the indigenous elite.

Western-style municipal government in Southeast Asia has followed a somewhat smoother course. For one thing, urbanization has been a very recent development and the direct outcome of Western penetration. Moreover, in the colonial areas, the town councils set up in the late nineteenth century were largely run by Europeans and for Europeans. Almost all their members were nominated by government, generally to represent special-interest groups, and an official majority dominated these councils. Similarly the local bodies that were wholly devised by the central authorities, such as the district organization of the Malay States, functioned with less dislocation of native life because they did not supplant indigenous institutions.

The interwar period witnessed an expansion, chiefly on

paper, of rural and urban governmental machinery, in partial fulfilment of pledges made under nationalist pressure for greater autonomy. In Burma, by the end of the 1920's, the number of municipalities had grown to fifty-eight, the proportion of elected members had increased, town residents were enfranchised on the basis of property qualifications, and the presidents of municipal councils were no longer appointed. Moreover, the responsibilities of town governments had been expanded to include vernacular education and slaughterhouse inspection in addition to their earlier supervision of police, roads, markets, and waterworks. Despite this enlargement of opportunities for urban self-government, Burmese town-dwellers remained indifferent and failed to utilize them.[1]

In rural Burma, an act passed in 1922 created twenty-eight district councils, comprising local officials and other members elected indirectly through Circle Boards, to serve without salary for a three-year term. Their responsibilities and revenues were similar to those of the municipal councils. The rural bodies thus created were artificial in that they bypassed rather than strengthened the village unit. Villages remained much the same as before, but the new councils increased the duties of provincial officials, hitherto responsible only for operating local funds. The post of district councillor went begging since it brought with it neither salary nor prestige and because council proceedings were conducted in Western style and dealt with matters in which the rural Burmese were not spontaneously interested. As things worked out, the district councils never became integrated with the village committees, to which sufficient powers were never delegated, and Circle Boards

[1] "Committees were careless in hiring employees and rarely punished maladministration even when fraud and loss of revenue were reported. Citizens complained but rarely used their elective power to place more responsible men on the councils." John Cady, "Burma," in *The Development of Self-Rule and Independence in Burma, Malaya, and the Philippines*, New York, 1948, p. 7.

served almost exclusively as electoral colleges for the district councils. Not only did the district councillors insist on retaining control of local funds but they failed to use them wisely in the people's interest. The Burma Constitution of 1935 did little to alter the structure or role of either urban or rural administrative bodies, and it paved the way for Burmese politicians to exercise their baneful influence on local government.[2]

In Indochina, French policy in regard to local government aimed at reproducing the highly centralized administration of France and also at modernizing and democratizing Vietnamese village life. The commune in Vietnam was probably the most uniform and autonomous village unit in pre-colonial Southeast Asia. Inspired by the agrarian ideals which they inherited from China, Vietnam's erstwhile overlord, the emperors of Annam had been willing to respect its independence because the commune assured an orderly and inexpensive local administration and because it was the agency through which new communes were created and agriculture expanded.[3] The strongly centralized bureaucracy which the French set up in Indochina at the turn of the century regarded the commune as an intolerable state within a state. So it proceeded to sap the commune's vitality by juxtaposing its own institutions with those of the indigenous village and mandarinate. At the same time the central government increased the collective responsibility of the commune in matters of tax collection, maintenance of order, and provision of military recruits. The French also rearranged village and cantonal boundaries, introduced the registration of vital statistics and land titles, intervened in the administration of justice, and reorganized the office of Notable. Thus the Council of Notables, originally drawn from among members of the

[2] Donnison, F. S. V., *Public Administration in Burma*, London, 1953, pp. 76–77.
[3] See Briffaut, C., *La Cité Annamite*, 3 vols., Paris, 1909–12.

village hierarchy, was saddled with onerous duties and deprived of many of its traditional powers. After 1920, when the French made the office of Notable elective for the purpose of giving non-taxpayers for the first time a voice in village administration and a means of redress against the Notables' abuse of power, very few of the authentic communal leaders were willing to run for office. Instead, they engineered the election of their own "straw men," whose moral influence locally was nil and whose only asset in French eyes was a certain familiarity with Western ways. Eventually the French perceived that their innovations in rural administration were a failure, and in 1941 the elective councils were abolished and their traditional prerogatives restored to the Notables.[4]

A somewhat similar evolution occurred, though for different reasons, in Indonesia, where the Village Act of 1906 was eventually abandoned.[5] Under its provisions all villages had been given a large and identical measure of autonomy with the aim of strengthening their internal solidarity. In practice, however, it was found that the success of this policy depended too much on the influence of the individual headman and that, contrary to the objective desired, his position had been gradually weakened rather than strengthened by conversion of what was essentially a social entity into an administrative unit. Moreover, few villages proved to be sufficiently evolved to cope with the elaborate Western system set up under the Act. So the Dutch reverted to the earlier method of governing through hereditary regents, who were advised by Dutch officials and provided with councils to help them handle village administration. Above the village system and integrated with it was a provincial administration, and in 1918 an

[4] Mus, Paul, "The Role of the Village in Vietnamese Politics," *Pacific Affairs*, Sept. 1949.
[5] Furnivall, J. S., *Memorandum on Reconstruction Problems in Burma*, New York, 1944, p. 30.

apex was provided for the structure in the form of the Volksraad, or People's Council.

Prompted by developments in neighboring colonies, the absolute monarchy of Thailand reorganized its local administration in the late nineteenth century. Thereafter the country was divided into circles, made up of provinces, which in turn were composed of districts. The smallest administrative unit was the village, of which a group formed the commune, and a number of communes, the district. Traditionally the headman was democratically elected by the villagers, though their choice had to be approved by the provincial governor. Neighboring headmen, in their turn, chose—subject to gubernatorial approval—an individual to head the commune and represent its villages. Disputes that could not be settled at the village or communal level were referred to the district officer, who occupied the lowest rung in the Thai service and acted as the provincial governor's deputy in his area.

In the interwar period, and particularly after the constitutional regime was established in 1932, controls over the rural administration were tightened by the central government and municipal administration was introduced. The circle was eliminated and the province, now placed directly under the Ministry of Interior, became the major administrative division of the country and also the unit for electing representatives to the National Assembly. While the provincial governors, hitherto virtually autonomous, were now made dependent on Bangkok, provincial and district councils were instituted in the name of democracy, though their composition and powers insured docility to local officialdom and national policy. Little change was made in the lowest rural administrative stratum, despite several unsuccessful attempts by National Assemblymen to transform the village and commune heads into salaried civil servants and to improve their training and manner of election. The central government, which opposed such moves, was nevertheless automatically altering the position and work of the communal heads by assuming more responsibility for the suppression of rural crime and by developing the means of communication. Furthermore, its refusal to permit the new provincial and district councils to discuss "policy" and its practice of making them almost wholly dependent financially upon sparse local contributions contributed to the failure of this experiment in rural government.

Nor did municipal innovations in Thailand fare much better. The leaders of the 1932 coup d'état created three types of self-governing municipalities, whereas prior to the constitutional regime only sanitary boards on the British model had existed in but a few of the larger Thai towns. All three types included an assembly, elected by the municipality to advise the municipal councillors, an administrative body composed of a president elected by the assembly, and a varying number of persons selected by him subject to the approval of the assembly and the provincial governor.[6] The over-large assemblies, made up of untrained and unpaid individuals chosen by a small and indifferent electorate, were given control of very limited local revenues to carry out their responsibilities for municipal sanitation, communications, water supply and social welfare. Their dependence on loans to supplement their meager revenues kept these assemblies in a state of subservience to the central and provincial governments, and little or nothing was done to help them with long-term planning or train them in efficient methods of municipal administration. In fact, at the outbreak of the Pacific War, only three city, eighty-two town, and thirty-three commune municipalities were functioning in Thailand.

In Malaya, particularly in the Straits Settlements, the development of strong municipal institutions offered a striking contrast to affairs in Thailand. Even in the peninsu-

[6] Reeve, W. D., *Public Administration in Siam*, London, 1951, p. 44.

lar states, large towns had been placed under sanitary boards, which were given charge of the usual spheres of municipal administration. Though they were composed of officials and of propertied individuals selected by the British government and outstanding economic groups and appointed by the sultan concerned, the large number of such bodies in so small a country as Malaya gave many persons experience in local administration. The ability they displayed and the power they wielded differed widely in the three major governmental units of Malaya. Both at the town and village levels, local self-government was more developed in the Federated than in the Unfederated States, and the port cities of the Straits Settlements outdistanced their inland colleagues in the competence with which they handled their responsibilities and in their independent attitude toward the colonial government.

Everywhere in Southeast Asia, but particularly in Malaya, such improvements in local government as occurred before World War II took place in the large towns where the European population was concentrated. Early attempts at reforming village administration were largely abandoned, and the local headmen, crushed by the burden of routine administrative duties, lost contact and therefore influence with the people under their leadership. Thus the great mass of the population remained either untouched or only indirectly affected by the centralizing influences that were rapidly transforming urban communities and local officialdom. At the provincial level, the expanding network of specialized services (such as public works, forestry, and the like) was extending the tentacles of the central government and was also increasing the number of officials, of whom there were now more natives than Europeans. Rising nationalism in the colonies and budgetary exigencies, particularly during the depression, made the employment of more indigenous talent imperative. European officials were consequently concentrated in the higher echelons and in urban offices. Development of the means of communication enabled them to make visits, when necessary, to outlying areas at high speed, and the advent of European women in increasing numbers created a social life from which Southeast Asians were largely excluded. Not only were European officials fewer and more aloof than before, but between them and the rural masses there grew up a barrier consisting of the new native officialdom. Centralization and an enlarged indigenous bureaucracy moved forward hand in hand.

The war and early postwar periods accentuated existing trends. The new national governments of the area naturally substituted native for European officials except in a handful of highly technical positions, and in the remaining colonies posts went begging for lack of European candidates willing to take up a career with such insecure prospects. The enormously swollen native bureaucracy suffered from the dearth of trained and experienced administrators, inadequate salaries, and the growth of corruption as a result of the Japanese occupation and the greater postwar opportunities for the abuse of public office. For the professional politicians, whose numbers multiplied rapidly with political independence, the task of pruning native officialdom was far harder than for colonial administrations not dependent upon popular votes.

Handicapped by an inadequate personnel and by a war-damaged economy and morale, the newly installed national governments were fighting for their lives, in some cases against their country's former rulers, and almost without exception against crime and armed revolt in rural areas. Under such circumstances the need to strengthen the central authority was obvious, but in some places it was literally impossible or politically unwise to do so. In all countries of the area regional feeling ran high and minority groups—both indigenous and alien—were strong. No country illustrates this fundamental dilemma better than Indonesia, which has the largest population, the most widely dispersed geographical area, and the strongest separatist tendencies and emotional schisms of any state in Southeast Asia.

INDONESIA

The postwar struggle between Indonesia and Holland for control of the archipelago ended in December 1949, with the emergence of a federal structure. Replacement of the federation—the Republic of the United States of Indonesia—by a "unitary" Republic of Indonesia in August 1950 signified an automatic increase in governmental centralization, which in turn heightened regional feeling, particularly in East Indonesia. To prevent regionalism from becoming separatism, and also to fulfil the democratic ideals on which the Republic was avowedly based, an increase in local autonomy was clearly indicated. All of independent Indonesia's successive governments have pledged greater local self-government on an elective basis but none has seemed able to fulfil the pledge. In addition to the above-mentioned difficulties common to all postwar Southeast Asia, Indonesia has suffered from lack of uniformity and stability in existing regional bodies, intrusion of party politics colored with religious extremism, and indecision at high levels as to the basic principles which should underlie regional and municipal machinery. Some of the regional governments date from the colonial era, others stem from postwar Dutch federalist projects, and still others were set up under the original Djogjakarta Republic. Not only does their structure—as regards both name and functions—lack uniformity, but there is considerable variation in the interpretation of their responsibilities and in their relation to the provincial administrations. Even the basic question as to how such bodies should be elected has remained unresolved, largely because of the rivalry in both rural and urban areas between Indonesia's two biggest political parties, the Partai Nasional Indonesia (PNI) and the Masjumi.

In 1948 a law was passed laying down the general lines of local government and providing for decentralization of power. This was later supplemented by provisional legislation for Java and parts of Sumatra. Indonesia was divided into ten provinces and the Special District of Djogjakarta; the provinces were divided into *kabupaten* (equivalent to prewar regencies) of which there are about 160, and large cities were given a status analogous to that of *kabupaten* in the administrative hierarchy; on a lower rung were placed the many small towns and innumerable villages.[7] Aside from the contemplated elimination of residencies and a few other units which, under the Dutch, had stood between the provinces and the regencies, this structure differed little from its predecessor. What was basically new was introduction of the elective principle at the town and *kabupaten* level, and a generally greater delegation of power to local bodies.

Application of the various local administration laws has run into serious snags, and elections have been held in only two places. Elsewhere local bodies resemble the national parliament in that their membership has been appointive on the basis of estimated party strength and of representation for minorities and other special-interest groups. The PNI, hoping to increase its membership in local bodies at the expense of its rival, the Masjumi, pressed hard for a revision of the law under which regional councils and assemblies had been set up. This was the issue on which the Natsir government fell in March 1951, but the law was not subsequently modified. Nor did the elections held at Minahassa in June and at Djogjakarta in August 1951, at both of which over seventy percent of the eligible electorate voted, alter the balance of power between the two

[7] See Finkelstein, L. S., "The Indonesian Federal Problem," *Pacific Affairs*, Sept. 1951.

major parties.[8] These elections appear to have served only a limited purpose either as precedents or as a basis for determining general principles for other local elections and for a clear-cut division of power between the central and regional administrations. Local autonomy seems to have laid down no strong roots above the village level, and such self-governing regional institutions as exist have been functioning far from smoothly.

Regional councillors and assemblymen complain that local interests lack proper representation; that officials sent out by Djakarta to the provinces are corrupt, inefficient, and too frequently rotated; and that the central government makes inadequate financial allocations and arbitrary decisions affecting them without knowledge of conditions in particular areas or consideration for regional feelings.[9] In short, they assert that their autonomy will remain merely nominal unless they receive adequate revenues and powers to carry out the responsibilities of local government. As proof of government indifference to their survival they point to the fact that no steps have been taken to replace or revive the Central Sumatra Legislative Assembly since its functioning was suspended in 1951.[10]

For its part the central government is discouraged by the instability of certain regional councils and resents the intrusion of some local councillors into its domain of policy-making. In the autumn of 1952, the regional councils or assemblies of the North Moluccas, West Java, and Minahassa decided independently to suspend sessions because of disagreements with other local authorities. Both the chairman of Parliament and that of the civil administration have complained that some of the provisional regional

[8] In highly literate and predominantly Christian Minahassa the PNI triumphed, whereas in largely illiterate and strongly Muslim Djogjakarta the Masjumi won out.
[9] *Christian Science Monitor*, April 1, 1953.
[10] *Times of Indonesia*, Djakarta, Dec. 31, 1952.

assemblies were not concentrating upon their "proper functions" and were too often acting like minor parliaments by discussing problems of high policy.[11] A recognized difficulty was that in Indonesia, contrary to the situation in neighboring countries, the chairman of a regional assembly was not the highest local official, and consequently disagreements between the two were not infrequent. Party politics were also hampering the development of local institutions. In Kalimantan (Borneo) conflicts between rival parties became so bitter that they actually prevented the government from setting up a legislative assembly for the area,[12] and as recently as January 1954 complaints were still being made to the central government regarding its failure to take any decisive action in the matter. More serious, political parties have seemed more intent on creating a following in the provinces than on educating the people in the selection of suitable representatives, and the government has been very dilatory in resolving the issue.[13]

At the village level there seems not to have been much change, except that the position of headman has progressively deteriorated. In October 1952 the Bandung branch of the Indonesia Village Administrators Association (PPDI) drew the government's attention to the difficult position of village chiefs, as regards both funds and security. Only fifteen to twenty percent of them, it claimed, could live on their personal incomes, the great majority being dependent on irregular local contributions or minuscule salaries of which only about half had actually been paid.[14] In September 1953 the Premier, in answer to fresh complaints from the Association of Village Administrators,

[11] Antara dispatches, Feb. 17 and March 11, 1953.
[12] *Times of Indonesia*, Feb. 20, 1953.
[13] Kahin, G. McT., "Indonesia's Strengths and Weaknesses," *Far Eastern Survey*, Sept. 26, 1951.
[14] *Times of Indonesia*, Oct. 28, 1952.

said that the long overdue improvement in their status must await promulgation of the law on regional autonomy currently under consideration.[15] Insecurity has been a particularly serious problem in West Java, where, between 1950 and 1953, 318 members of village administrations were killed by armed gangs.[16] In April 1953, several organizations of village chiefs in Java asked the government to declare such bandits "enemies of the state" and to permit an expansion and integration of village defense corps. The PPDI took this occasion to suggest specific political ways of restoring law and order and of achieving closer collaboration between villagers and their administration. In particular, the government was urged to speed up the holding of elections to village assemblies and to foster democratic practices indirectly by refraining from issuing directives that should more properly emanate from the villagers themselves.[17]

Municipal bodies, despite their long experience with self-government and their more highly qualified membership, have not been much better off. The Djakarta authorities have been able to reach no basic decision as to the optimum form of city government, as between a centralized power or a board of management. Municipal councillors themselves have complained about the inadequacy of their funds and the unrepresentative nature of their membership. In November 1951 the Djakarta Council voted itself out of existence and asked that it be replaced by an elective body.[18] Three months later the Bandung Council followed suit.

Almost a year later, on February 17, 1953, Antara news agency reported that the Ministry of Interior was at long

[15] *Ibid.,* Sept. 17, 1953.
[16] Antara dispatch, April 25, 1953.
[17] Antara dispatches, April 11, 25, 27, 1953.
[18] *Report on Indonesia,* Indonesian Information Office, New York, Nov. 8, 1951.

last drafting legislation that would create by stages a uniform structure for regional assemblies throughout Indonesia and that, on an experimental basis, a large share of autonomy would be accorded to at least one village in each province.[19] In December 1953 this draft bill was referred to a special committee for further study. In view of the experimental nature of this new program and the admittedly provisional nature of the legislation proposed, many years will probably elapse before the great majority of Indonesians can try their hand at making the machinery of local democracy work.

BURMA

The government of independent Burma, which was faced with a series of armed revolts within three months of its formation, has had little time or energy to devote to administrative reforms. Perforce the old order was retained, and though the provincial officialdom became almost wholly Burmese, the people showed little more confidence in them than in their predecessors. This was due in part to an ingrained Burmese distrust of official authority and in part to the character and attitude of the civil service. In common with other countries of the area, Burma has suffered from a lack of competent, honest, and experienced native officials, but it has the additional handicap of a civil service that showed itself politically ambitious and irresponsible in the pressures it put on the central government during a period of grave emergency. Moreover, party politics have hampered the work of rural officials and the functioning of local administrative bodies,[20] for the struggle between the dominant party (AFPFL) and opposition groups has not been confined to the national arena. In the war-damaged capital of Burma, rehabilitation has been

[19] *Times of Indonesia,* March 13, 1953.
[20] Cady, John, "The Situation in Burma," *Far Eastern Survey,* April 22, 1953.

held up by a conflict of authority between the AFPFL-dominated Corporation and the Rangoon Development Trust. And in the Pegu elections of March 1953, a meeting called to choose the president of that municipality had to adjourn without coming to any decision because, as one Burmese daily quaintly put it, "the councillors were politically-minded."[21]

Complaints about this state of affairs were frequently voiced by the people, but it was not until 1951 that the government felt itself strong enough to undertake the reform of local administration. A committee set up at that time drafted a program after three years of study, but even before its proposals were officially announced several experiments in increasing local autonomy had already been made. The Democratization of Local Administration Act, presented as part of the Union Welfare scheme (Pyidawtha) in August 1952, sought to remove the bureaucratic machinery for government and substitute a large measure of rural autonomy in order to re-establish contact between the mass of the people and the central authorities.[22] It provides for five types of administrative unit—village, town, township, district and Union—all of whose governing bodies are to be elected either by popular vote or by a system of representation from one to the next. Clearly defined administrative, judicial, and fiscal powers are vested in the local bodies, and the villagers are to have police and defense units as well as courts provided with competence in both civil and criminal cases. Voting in elections to the village council and to ward committees in the cities is made compulsory for every adult resident national. In order to safeguard public interests, members of local bodies are made subject to dismissal for specified sins of commission and omission; a people's advocate is to be appointed in

[21] *The Burman,* Rangoon, March 24, 1953.
[22] See articles by Kyipwayay Oo Thein in *The Burman,* July 3, 1951 and Aug. 9, 1952.

every district; and the President of the Union of Burma is empowered to suspend or withdraw the charter from any local body or to remove any of its members for just cause. To enable rural autonomy to function, each township is allotted kyat 50,000, which can be used at its discretion for carrying out schemes initiated by its welfare committee. Supplementary funds, if required, must be raised through public contributions.

Experimental application of this law early in 1952 to "suitable areas with selected official personnel" disclosed a number of weaknesses. Law and order were far from restored throughout Burma, and the medley of new councils bewildered the people and added to the burdens of the already overworked local officials. By December 1952 the government had decided to establish a special ministry to assist in applying the Local Administration Act. A whole year was to elapse before further progress was announced. In the interval, the new ministry conducted special training classes for the personnel who would help in applying the plan during 1954 to four areas—Kyaukse, Meiktila, Insein and Kyaukpyu.

Some Burmans, however, still believe that the fundamental trouble has to do less with the practical difficulties encountered in carrying out the Act than with the principles and assumptions underlying it.[23] It was said that the people had given no evidence of being ripe, or eager, for greater local autonomy and that the scheme was essentially unworkable because it had been imposed from above. Moreover, serious discrepancies existed between the government's theory and practice. No one seriously doubted the sincerity of Premier Nu's desire to train the Burmese people in democratic practices, but did not such devices as compulsory voting and continued governmental interven-

[23] See *The Burman*, Sept. 27, Dec. 2, 1952, and *The Burmese Review*, Rangoon, Dec. 29, 1952.

tion in local and municipal administration savor of the traditional paternalism and authoritarianism?[24]

VIETNAM

The postwar evolution of self-governing institutions in rural Vietnam has followed a course contrary to that elsewhere in Southeast Asia, with the possible exception of that part of central Burma which has similarly been in the hands of militant Communists. In both areas the old officialdom has been swept away and local administration has been drastically transformed to conform to the Soviet model and to the exigencies of guerrilla warfare. Thus in Vietnam and central Burma it is no longer the towns, now generally outside of Communist control, but rather the villages which have become revolutionary centers.[25] The traditionally conservative Vietnamese commune has undergone a profound change, although the laws governing it were enacted nominally to safeguard and even reinforce its pre-colonial autonomy.[26] In contrast, the main cities are run either by provisional committees or by prefectorial administrations nominated by the French, although drawn increasingly from the Vietnamese community. In both cases, however, the control from above has been tighter, and it is noteworthy that Premier Tam's policy statement for the Bao Dai regime in June 1952 called for administrative reforms, including decentralization.[27] In January 1953 elections were held in the main towns and a few villages con-

[24] In 1949 the cabinet appointed its own candidate to fill the seat of an elected Rangoon municipal councillor, whose election had been nullified by the High Court. In a broadcast appealing for public cooperation in carrying out the Local Administration Act, the Premier gave specific instructions to townships as to how they should use the funds allotted them presumably for schemes which they themselves were to have originated. *The Burman*, July 3, 1951; Jan. 8, 1953.
[25] Mus, *loc. cit.*
[26] "La République Démocratique du Vietnam," in *La Vérité sur le Vietnam*, Paris, 1947.
[27] Associated Press dispatch, June 22, 1952.

trolled by the French Union forces, but the franchise was so restricted and the area involved so small that the results were regarded as insignificant. These elections were to have been the forerunner of elections to provincial assemblies, but the war situation and the far more momentous negotiations between the Vietnam State and France for a new treaty relationship have forced the shelving of any further advance towards local government reform.

An interesting development that partially paralleled the squatter resettlement program in Malaya and that, it was thought, might leave a permanent imprint on the delta areas of north Vietnam was the formation in 1951–52 of some two hundred GAMOs (*Groupement Administratif Mobile Opérationnel*). These were composed of engineers, Vietnamese local government officials, and French military and civilian officers, who closely followed the French Union combat forces. In areas they had taken back from the Vietminh, the attempt was made by the GAMOs to revive the economic, political, and social life of the village. (The GAMO has been described as an administrative shock unit comparable to that of mobile combat troops.) Within a very short time, the GAMO tried to reinstate the village chiefs, reconstitute the Councils of Notables, reopen communications and markets, and organize the villagers for their own defense. Temporarily, the GAMO also acted as a liaison unit between the reconstituted village and the central administration.[28] The first of such groups set up at Haiduong in 1952 was reported to be doing satisfactorily.

Far more profound and radical has been the evolution of local government in the Vietminh-held areas.[29] An early law of the "Democratic Republic of Vietnam" replaced the colonial administrative machinery with an organization based on a pyramid network of people's committees.

[28] *Le Monde*, July 26, 1952.
[29] See analysis by Bernard Fall, "Local Administration under the Viet-Minh," *Pacific Affairs*, March 1954.

Such committees were instituted at all levels—communal, regional, provincial and municipal, as well as in the three main divisions of Vietnam—and were supplemented vertically by other committees established for vocational or other special-interest groups. The whole structure was closely integrated: control over each stratum was exercised by the committee immediately superior to it, culminating in the cabinet and its executive bodies. All of the people's committees were elected by direct universal adult suffrage, regardless of literacy or other qualifications, with the exception of certain municipalities which were placed under appointive committees.[30] But within less than a year and before the Republic lost control of the main cities of Vietnam, a change was made in the reconstructed administrative system. In the interests of simplification and economy, the canton was eliminated and neighboring villages were grouped together in single administrative units. This step reduced the communes in the delta to one-fourth and those in the uplands to one-half of their original numbers,[31] and thinned the ranks of local officialdom.[32] Of the 3,000 functionaries in Annam, 2,000 were dismissed, and many of those remaining served, either perforce or from patriotism, for little more than their food, clothing, and shelter. Eligibility requirements for both voters and membership in the People's Committees were liberally interpreted, but the tasks and responsibilities devolving upon these committees were so onerous and their domination by military exigencies so great that the populace lost its initial enthusiasm for elections and the holding of membership office. This set-up had the undoubted advantage of permitting the Republic to achieve a far greater centralization

[30] *Quelques aspects du Vietnam nouveau*, Hanoi, 1946.
[31] Vo Nguyen Giap, *One Year of Revolutionary Achievement*, Bangkok, Oct. 1946.
[32] See article by P. Devillers in *Une Semaine dans le Monde*, Paris, June 22, 1946.

of power than had been dreamed of under French rule, and it also facilitated the propagation of Marxism and the conduct of prolonged warfare. But its disadvantages were apparently felt to be great enough to cause a slight change of policy on the part of the central government. Late in 1952 popular assemblies were reportedly reconstituted in a modified version of their original form, prior to their war-inspired integration with the military commands. Whatever their final fate the Republic has at least succeeded, as Mr. Fall points out, in establishing the substructure of what could become a decentralized "democratic" government (in the Communist sense of the word), though obviously only if the Communist leaders permit such a development.

MALAYA

As for Malaya, unique demographic and economic conditions have given the small Crown Colony of Singapore Island so special a character and such a top-heavy and costly administration as to make its evolution largely irrelevant for comparison with local government developments elsewhere in Southeast Asia. Nevertheless its experience has served to influence somewhat the way in which greater local autonomy has been introduced in the neighboring Federation of Malaya, particularly as regards municipal administration.

In 1948 the introduction of elections for a minority of Singapore's legislative councillors preceded by some months the first elections for some of the town's municipal commissioners, and more stringent qualifications were originally required of voters for the latter than for the former. In both cases the franchise was confined to British subjects—a small minority of the population—and only slight public interest was shown in the elections. Slowly political parties began to take root in Singapore and developed along non-communal lines, but councillors have remained amateurs since the fee they receive for their public service has been too small to attract professional politicians. Perhaps as a consequence of a subsequent increase in the proportion of elected to nominated councillors, greater public interest has been shown in Singapore's elections. Yet, as of July 1953, only 77,000 out of a total population of nearly one million were eligible to vote and by no means all of these bothered to register on the electoral rolls. In 1950 Singapore was accorded the status of a City, and since that time there has been a growing though not insistent demand that all of its councillors and a mayor should be elected.[33] In 1951 a British expert called in by the Colony government to streamline Singapore's cumbersome and archaic municipal administration proposed certain measures of decentralization, including the creation of local administrative bodies in sizable population centers throughout the island.

Because of the Communist revolt on the Malayan mainland, local elections in the Federation were delayed until 1951, and then were confined to town boards in only a few of the largest towns. Qualifications for those wishing to vote for twelve out of Kuala Lumpur's eighteen municipal commissioners were so stringent that only a very small proportion of the almost 300,000 residents of the federal capital have been enfranchised, and only 7,250 persons registered on its electoral rolls.[34] Malacca, after accepting a municipal franchise, failed to use it; no elections were held there because all nine candidates for the municipal commission were returned unopposed. Penang, however, displayed lively interest in its elections. Three municipal elections in Johore occurred in 1953, and that state has led

[33] In April 1953 the Singapore government announced that it had accepted the principle of an elected mayor for the colony, to be chosen from among members of the city council or from among these eligible to be elected councillors.

[34] *Straits Times,* Singapore, Jan. 22, 1952; Sept. 23, 1953.

the way in popularly elected government on the peninsula. The gradual transformation of more than eighty town boards in the Federation into partially elected municipal commissions is envisaged for the near future.[35]

Little difficulty is foreseen in transforming gradually Malaya's town boards into popularly elected bodies. Elections held to date have been exemplary for the calm and orderly atmosphere in which they took place. Though the state councils have always retained the power to override town board decisions, it has rarely been exercised, for the local government bodies have generally been content not to intervene in the formulation of high policy. More serious has been the financial dependency on the central institutions, which have, as elsewhere in Southeast Asia, had the controlling power through allocation of the funds required to supplement the inadequate rates and fees collected by local bodies. A recent move on the part of the federal government aims, in principle, to grant financial autonomy to the newly elected town boards. But, as was pointed out in a report of the federal Committee on Town and Rural Board Finances, the practical results of such a move would depend on two factors—the willingness of the electorate to make financial sacrifices for the sake of increased local self-government, and the resources of the individual area concerned.

In Malaya's rural areas the resettlement of Chinese squatters, involving one-fourth of the Federation's population, has stimulated a reorganization of village administration for the Malays as well. The new villages inhabited by Chinese have been provided with councils (as well as modern amenities) in the hope that such opportunities for self-government and improved living conditions will offset the Communist propaganda to which the squatters had been exposed. Not unnaturally the Malays have coveted analo-

[35] G. Hawkins, "First Steps in Malayan Local Government," *Pacific Affairs*, June 1953.

gous improvements for their settlements. The Rural and Industrial Development Authority (RIDA), established in 1950 under the chairmanship of the Malays' outstanding leader, Dato Onn bin Jaafar, and provided with a fund of Str. $5 million, regards self-help by Malay villagers as its basic force. RIDA also aims to restore to local headmen their influence as traditional village leaders.[36] But it has not been able to accomplish much because the Malay state governments have lacked both qualified development officers and the requisite enthusiasm, and in the villages there has been more criticism of individual headmen than appreciation by the villagers of the principle of self-help. In the meantime, Johore, politically the most progressive state in the peninsula, produced in September 1951 a scheme calling for the election of headmen and for a pay scale sufficiently high to attract educated men willing to forego urban employment and public-spirited enough to make a lifetime career in one rural post.[37] For several years the British have been trying to strengthen the position of the headman, as the key to rural progress throughout the Federation. Headmen have received special training and have been encouraged to hold monthly meetings with their assistants and to attend regular conferences with the district officer and their colleagues. Their courts have been left unchanged in a reorganization which has made the judicial system more centralized. The most radical step of all, and one subject to considerable criticism, has involved making the post of headman permanent in order to give its holder continuity in office.[38] In December 1953 it was even proposed that the government should reserve a seat for *penghulus* on the Federal Legislative Council, but to date no action has been taken in regard to this suggestion.

[36] Charles Gamba and Ungku Aziz, "RIDA and Local Government," *Far Eastern Survey*, Oct. 10, 1951.
[37] *Straits Times*, Sept. 28, Oct. 6, 1951
[38] Jones, S. W., *Public Administration in Malaya*, London, 1953, p. 190.

In making these changes the federal government not only drew on its experience in setting up the new squatter villages but also sought the advice of a British expert in local government, Harold Bedale. A Village Council Ordinance was drafted in the spring of 1952 which gave considerable power over local affairs to villages selected by the state rulers and the British High Commissioner, but made them subject to the almost autocratic authority of the district officers. Before approving this bill, the Federal Council reduced the wide powers of district officers, and changed the name of the ordinance to Local Council Ordinance in order to make it applicable to both village and purely rural areas, fixed the term of office for local councillors at three years, increased the minimum size of local councils to seven, and gave their members greater leeway in the preparation of budgets. Because the creation of village councils is far less complicated than the transformation of town boards—particularly as regards the qualifications for electors—it was hoped that by the end of that year about two hundred local councils (as compared with some twenty town boards) would have been formed.[39] The Bedale Report, made public in early 1953, strongly recommended the establishment of a special department to handle local government matters because of the difficulties involved in building from the ground up in an area where such institutions had no strong roots and which was plagued by armed insurrection.

THAILAND

The decline of local government institutions, both rural and urban, which began in Thailand during the war, has now apparently entered the final stages. Disintegration set in during the Japanese occupation, when headmen ceased to be elected by villagers and were appointed by district

[39] *Straits Times,* May 9, July 4, 1952; Jan. 14, 1953.

officers, subject to the provincial commissioner's approval. The provincial assemblies, instituted in 1938 as popularly elected bodies and as checks on the power of district officers and provincial officials, never received the funds required for local development projects. Also during the war, an act was passed which strengthened the power of the central government at the expense of municipal assemblies and councils.

After the Japanese surrender, the Free Thai government proposed various ways of restoring local autonomy,[40] but its plans came to nothing, for corruption at high levels remained unchecked and no provision was made for delegating wider powers to local bodies. Since the great bulk of rural and municipal revenues continued to be drained into the national treasury—to which application had to be made for funds to carry out local government—town and rural administrations were unable to undertake rehabilitation schemes, let alone long-term planning.

Civilian promoters of the coup d'état which displaced the Free Thai government in November 1947 made a brave effort to clean up the prevailing corruption. But the suits brought against a few officials and the wholesale transfer of thirty-one provincial commissioners and of one hundred and fifty lesser provincial executives did not attack the root cause of the evil and, moreover, smacked of party politics. Under the military regime which came to power in April 1948, corruption has flourished on an unprecedented scale. The spoils system has operated unchecked in the appointment of high officials, in both provinces and municipalities, while the armed forces and military police have increased their power throughout the country at the expense of both appointed and elected civilian officials.

Political patronage, however, has been a less disruptive force in Thai rural and urban administration than the direct pressure brought to bear on local officials by the

[40] *Bangkok Post*, Aug. 28, 1946; Feb. 11, 1947.

party in power, and this has been true of all Thailand's postwar governments. In the elections of August 1946 the Pridi cabinet circularized provincial officials in favor of government candidates. In 1949 and in 1950, high officials of the Pibun administration were accused during successive election campaigns of threatening officials with dismissal or transfer if they did not come out in support of their party's candidates.[41] The government itself opposed in Parliament a proposal to revive election of headmen, claiming that "since village chiefs have the status of assistants to civil officials, it is technically right that they be nominated by those officials rather than elected by the people."[42] More recently, in September 1953, the government turned down a proposal made in the National Assembly to make the post of provincial governor elective. An Administrative Act of February 1952 did increase the executive powers of the provincial commissioners vis-à-vis their subordinates, and foreshadowed the establishment of provincial budgets, but the governors remained subservient to the Ministry of Interior, and the rural police and armed forces still escaped their control. Ten months later a complete reorganization of rural administration was announced. To deal more effectively with the "Communist threat," the government decided to place "strong men" in strategic provincial posts,[43] and in April 1953 all provincial commissioners were ordered to make daily radio reports to the Ministry of Interior.[44] In the preceding month, all provincial assemblies were abolished. No elections to them had been held since 1943; they had met very rarely; and they had possessed neither power nor funds. On the ground that they were both useless and expensive, their elimination appeared to be reasonable. But no more functional or

[41] *Ibid.*, June 23, 1947; Jan. 3, 1951.
[42] *Ibid.*, Aug. 8, 1950.
[43] *Ibid.*, Dec. 27, 1952.
[44] *Ibid.*, April 22, 1953.

practical machinery for rural local government took their place and, at the same time, municipal self-government in Thailand was dealt a severe blow.

For many years Thai municipal administrations have been charged with inefficiency and corruption. Late in 1948 the government drafted a bill designed to create a city-manager form of government, provide municipalities with new sources of income, raise the qualifications for candidates for municipal office, and reduce the size of municipal assemblies and the number of their employees. This proposal trod on too many important toes, and parliamentary opposition became so strong that the government had to defer action on the bill.

Meanwhile Thailand's two largest cities, Bangkok and Thonburi, suffered from travesties of modern urban administration. Their assemblymen bickered and intrigued, and either boycotted meetings or broke them up by their rowdy behavior. Mayors came and went: some resigned because of inability to carry out their mandates; others were ousted on charges of incompetence or corruption. Bangkok's last and most eccentric elected mayor, Khun Lert, alternately feuded with his assembly and officials, and launched futile campaigns against abuses of both a serious and a foolish nature. In March 1953, after the office of mayor had been shorn of its few remaining executive powers, Khun Lert was dismissed by the Ministry of Interior from the post to which he had been elected, without even observing the formality of preferring charges. This humiliating finale to the democratic administration of the capital city followed by two months the passage of a Municipal Reform Act, which represented a retrogression in the sphere of local government analogous to that which had overtaken the national political scene.

The Municipal Reform Act provides for the appointment of mayors and closer control of city and town municipalities by the provincial governors, who are empowered to dismiss mayors and any of their councillors as well as to dissolve municipal assemblies. District officers receive similar authority over village municipalities. Furthermore, for a ten-year period, the Minister of Interior—that is, the political party in power—will appoint half of the members of municipal assemblies, thus duplicating on the municipal level the procedure prevailing in the National Assembly. Considerable opposition to this change was shown even by members of the pro-government parties, and a government official saw fit to "order" supporters of the administration in the National Assembly to run as candidates for the municipal elections which took place throughout the kingdom on May 17, 1953.[45] Two months later the then Minister of Education was named Mayor of Bangkok, and that municipality (as well as neighboring Thonburi) was promised additional revenues and more financial autonomy. In Bangkok only 22 percent of the eligible electors voted; all of the municipal assemblymen elected belonged to the pro-government "Strength of Twelve Group"; and even over their protests, General Mangkorn Promyothi, Minister of Education, was named mayor of Bangkok.

In view of Thailand's unique status, the fate which has overtaken its local government institutions is tragic. However, it is only the most extreme, as well as the most discouraging, example of the failure of analogous institutions throughout Southeast Asia. National governments, which have in theory grasped the desirability of more responsible urban and rural autonomy, have been no more successful than colonial regimes in securing the popular cooperation essential for such a system. The new class of professional politicians is still afraid to undertake drastic reform of the overstaffed and underpaid bureaucracy, but Southeast Asian governments have taken two forward steps since the war. All have agreed to the elective principle for public office and, in very recent months, to that of wider local

[45] *Ibid.*, March 6, 1953.

financial autonomy. However, permitting local bodies to use local resources for their own development projects does not solve the problem for impoverished areas. On the constructive side it does permit local bodies to gain experience in handling their own affairs and, above all, it places squarely on the people responsibility for financing what they want done in and for their own communities.

Wartime and postwar developments have greatly sharpened political consciousness among the masses, but not to the point where they seem to appreciate how elective local government can be made to serve their collective welfare. They have not been slow to complain of maladministration, but to them this means the abuse of office by individual officials or the neglect of their interests by the central government, to which they continue to look for the remedy. In every country of the area the machinery for greater local autonomy has been provided by the central government, but nothing further is likely to be accomplished until the people realize its potential usefulness to themselves and accept the responsibilities which it imposes.

CHAPTER SEVEN

Conclusion

THE MOST FUNDAMENTAL fact of Southeast Asia today is that it is engaged in revolutions which can by no means be assumed to have run their course. If the Philippines, Indonesia, and Burma have achieved the somewhat uneasy independence which Thailand never wholly lost, the social revolution in those countries, save as it was accomplished as a by-product of colonialism, has hardly begun, and there lies ahead the vast and complex task of adaptation to independence in the modern world. In such circumstances, where sheer survival is the first criterion of success, it would be absurd to set too high expectations for representative government. Even apart from the particular difficulties and hindrances which exist in the Southeast Asian countries it must be recognized that democracy no longer has the same clear and unequivocal support which it had in the latter part of the nineteenth century when it was obviously the way of progress and enlightenment. There is now the challenge of Fascism in one or another variant, even though the term itself has become unfashionable, and Communism holds out the tempting myth of proletarian dictatorship which puts an end to all ills.

Although it can be a matter for elaborate and heated argument, there seems to be good reason to accept the conclusion that, except on the local level, democratic institutions have not been traditionally known in Southeast

Asia, where government has been something embodied in and run by the few far above the heads of the mass of the people. The existence of democracy in the village is undoubtedly better than the existence of no democracy at all, but it is open to grave question whether this local democratic experience can be translated in any direct fashion to the national scene or to significantly larger social units than those to which it has in the past applied. In some part at least the answer must depend upon the answer to the further question as to whether the traditional village democracy is based upon the concept of the equality and dignity of man, which finds political expression in the principle of "one man, one vote," or whether it is rather the expression of the peculiar and intimate ties which knit together the people of a small and old-established community in which everyone knows everyone else and each person, as member of family and clan, has his fixed and organic place in the communal pattern. On the latter hypothesis it is rather the element of membership and status in the particular society which justifies participation in the democratic process than mere existence as an individual entitled to political rights and consideration.

In some measure of abstraction the national community has a similar conception of the close-knit belonging together of its members, but in actual fact the difference between it and the traditional village community is of very much the same order and almost as great as that between the earlier traditional economy and the modern impersonal money economy. To extend democracy from the local face-to-face relationship to the great national scene of unknown masses of men may well prove not in fact to be an extension at all but the introduction of a new and quite different principle. On this basis it might be possible to build an argument for a system of indirect elections which would rest upon the village communities as the foundation of the pyramid, but the peak would be so far removed from the

CONCLUSION

base as to run the danger of eliminating virtually all sense of direct popular participation.

On the whole it appears wiser not to seek to justify the new democratic institutions as something welling up from the people and their traditions but rather to acknowledge that these institutions are an alien importation which, if they are to survive, must adapt themselves to the special needs and backgrounds of the area. As an historical fact representative government has come to Southeast Asia as a continuation and aftermath of the impact of Western imperialism. In part, perhaps, its prestige derives from the fact that it is the form of government of the most successful imperial powers, who were the victors in two world wars, and its forms, if not its substance, have been adopted in the other great power bloc beyond the iron curtain; but presumably the most significant element in its immediate appeal is that it is the one type of free modern political structure of which the leaders and in lesser measure the peoples have had some experience. In colonial areas advance toward full control of the society by representative bodies was made the measure of the gradual approach to emancipation. To nationalist leaders the achievement of full-blown representative government became almost synonymous with the achievement of independence, and it is these leaders, themselves the product of the imperialist era, who have made the choice as to the type of political institutions the peoples of Southeast Asia should have as the first fruits of independence.

The inspiration for representative government came from the West but, as has frequently been pointed out, the circumstances under which it is being introduced in Asia are very different from those of its point of origin. In the West the transition from autocracy to democracy was a slow and gradual process, carried through in a far less complicated world than the present one. The piecemeal enfranchisement of segments of the population in a rough way kept pace with the evolution of a new economic and social life and with the spread of mass education and literacy. In Southeast Asia, the modern world has come with a rush and there has been no time for the kind of slow adaptation to new circumstances which was generally characteristic of the West. Although the colonial regimes introduced representative institutions of varying degrees of significance, they actually brought the mass of the people, with the partial exception of the Philippines, very little in the way of effective experience of the democratic process above a more or less local level. With the disappearance of the colonial regimes, all barriers were immediately pulled down and full political responsibility was vested, at least nominally, in the people at large. But the achievement of independence and of democratic constitutions does not change the fact that the great majority of the newly sovereign people still have only a meager approach to literacy and presumably even less of a knowledge of the great society to which they are now directly linked, the mediating role of the colonial power having been discarded. The actual management of political affairs may still rest with an elite comparable in its fashion to that which took the first steps toward representative institutions in the West, but the mass of the people has been enfranchised at a far earlier stage in its development.

At the minimum level of survival the new governments have done considerably better than the more pessimistic prophets were prepared to give them credit for. It is obvious, for instance, that nationalism has penetrated far too deeply to make possible any such reversal of history as was implied in the belief of some of the Dutch that the inability of the Indonesians to run their country would shortly lead the simple and trusting populace to repudiate the upstart leaders who had betrayed them and call back their former masters to restore the good old days. It is clear on the record that the governments have not collapsed or

CONCLUSION

disintegrated despite the fact that they have faced difficulties which would challenge the abilities of the most stable, mature, and experienced peoples. Burma with its confused jumble of civil strife came the nearest to disintegration but pulled itself back from disaster and now slowly approaches unity under a government which appears to have a real respect for the popular will. In both Indonesia and Burma it has been possible to draw upon the first rush of enthusiasm for new national governments and upon that revolutionary elan which Sukarno declares to be ebbing away in his country, but it is highly questionable that these can be counted on as continuing sources of strength and inspiration.

Up to now it is certainly true that the new governments have been able to draw and rely upon the remaining, but inevitably dwindling, momentum of the colonial systems. Even with the break brought by the intervening Japanese occupation the great bulk of the men and women who carry on the work of government in Indonesia and Burma are still the products of the colonial era, whether as its servants or its opponents. The present and prospective future shortages of trained manpower are all the more serious in view of the plans of the governments not merely to carry on at the margin of survival but to build modern societies with rising standards of living, provision for social welfare, and the technical devices for efficient production, transportation, and communications. The apparatus of the modern social welfare state is highly complex and expensive and requires for its effective operation a very large body of skilled experts and administrators whom it will be difficult to come by in societies in which the mass of the people continue to live just over the level of subsistence.

To bring even the necessities of modernity, let alone its more advanced conveniences and facilities, to the workers of the cities and the peasants of remote and scattered villages is a task of appalling magnitude, and will demand the training and proper utilization of far larger bodies of civil servants than the colonial administrations even began to dream of providing. It will be a major test of the leadership which has taken over to see whether or not it can bring forward the trained personnel which its programs demand if they are to be translated from paper to working reality.

Thus far there has been survival and some measure of reconstruction and advance, but there is also much which raises skepticism for the future. It appears to be generally conceded that the withdrawal of American control from the Philippines worked on the whole to produce a lowering of political morale and administrative efficiency, and in Indonesia the ending of Dutch rule has had a similar effect. No hasty conclusions should be drawn from this present deterioration because it is only reasonable to assume that there should be a difficult period of transition from the colonial relationship in which all ultimate authority and most of the top posts were in the hands of aliens and the taking over of power by nationals inexperienced in political management at the level of decision and command. In addition to the necessity of bringing forward a new top leadership, which now had to substitute responsibility for its former role of nationalist opposition, there was also inevitably some basic change in political values and orientation which could scarcely be carried through without fumbling and loss of motion.

For the longer pull judgment must obviously be suspended until we can see the form and substance of the new regimes after they have had a chance to become firmly established on their own. Nor, of course, can it be ignored that in the eyes of the people concerned, the lowering of standards and the losses in administrative efficiency may be far more than compensated for by the gain in national self-esteem and in the ability to determine the course the national government should pursue.

On the always dangerous ground of analogy with what

seem to be roughly similar circumstances elsewhere it is hard to avoid somewhat pessimistic forecasts for Southeast Asia in the decades which lie immediately ahead.[1] With the partial exception of Japan and Turkey, the record of representative institutions and of large-scale sustained economic and social advance among non-European peoples is a surprisingly meager and barren one, lending little encouragement to the naive belief that all that is needed to bring democracy and prosperity is to put an end to colonialism. It may be that such analogies are irrelevant, but it is not easy to identify the features which distinguish Southeast Asia from other apparently comparable areas in Asia, the Near and Middle East, and at least the more tropical parts of Latin America. In these areas the adoption of democratic constitutions has not prevented the actual drift of governments in the direction of dictatorship or oligarchy, standards of living have remained very low for the bulk of the population, and economic development has not only been hesitant and spotty but frequently associated with the activities of alien concerns. The control of these societies, and the wealth associated with it, have tended to remain in the hands of the few at the top. The strong man and often the military have had more or less undisputed sway, and changes in the government in power have normally reflected less the will of the people than a palace revolution in which one or another faction of the ruling clique has taken over. In fact almost everywhere except in those parts of the world in the temperate zones inhabited primarily by peoples of European descent the lethargy of stagnation has proved an effective barrier to the dynamic sweep of modern progress on Western European or American lines.

It requires no judgment as to whether progress of this variety is ultimately to be regarded as good or evil, de-

[1] See Rupert Emerson, "Progress in Asia: A Pessimistic View," *Far Eastern Survey*, Aug. 27, 1952.

sirable or undesirable, to determine the fact that very different modes and tempos of life have developed in different parts of the world. In the last few years there has been a growing assumption both that economic development can be greatly hastened by outside technical assistance and financial aid and that such development will work to establish the necessary underpinnings of democracy, but what the economic, social, and political effects will actually be remains to be seen.

Within Southeast Asia the two countries which because of their larger and longer experience with self-government can be drawn upon to furnish some possible clues as to the future destiny of their neighbors are Thailand and the Philippines. Since the development of the Philippines has already been commented on at some length it is unnecessary to do more than suggest some summary generalizations at this point. It must be recognized that comparison with other countries of the area may be misleading at some points because of the longer and more intensive experience of colonialism, the American effort to hasten the development of representative government and independence, and the general acceptance of Christianity. In the turn of political events under the Commonwealth and since independence there is much which is reminiscent of the political history of Latin American countries, but there is no easy means to determine whether this is the result of the common Spanish heritage or whether in both it is essentially other factors which are involved.

At all events the democracy of the Philippines of the last decade or so has left much to be desired. It is doubtful whether the man in the street and the village has felt any very active sense of participation in national politics, and, as was indicated earlier, the president has succeeded in drawing large powers to himself. There have been many charges of electoral malpractice, and corruption has been widespread. The Bell Report indicated the great gap between programs and achievements, particularly in the economic sphere, and pointed out a substantial number of reforms which needed to be undertaken governmentally and otherwise if the islands were to be put on a sound and progressive footing.

On the other hand, it is clear that more than the bare forms of representative institutions have survived. The elected assemblies play a real role, political parties vie with each other for the control of the government (even though the parties are not without their seamy side) and there is a wide measure of freedom of speech and press. The Philippines can certainly not be put forward as any model of the perfect constitutional and democratic society, but at the same time they have retained more in the way of both constitutionalism and democracy than many other states. Under the old political regime, beginning with Quezon, there was a tendency toward an oligarchical and inefficient system which could easily verge into the Central American pattern; to stem the drift it will be necessary to broaden the political base and draw in some new and vigorous blood. It may be that Ramon Magsaysay will prove to be the leader who can reverse the recent unfortunate trends— but there is also the possibility that he will become the strong man, the man on horseback, whose coming could prove no great surprise in the Philippine setting.

It is tempting and, within limits, justifiable to seek to utilize the experience of Thailand as a guide to what may be expected elsewhere in Southeast Asia under conditions of independence, but precisely the fact that the Thai people have not been through the mill of colonial rule casts suspicion on any effort to draw too close parallels. Experimentation with representative institutions has been under way in Thailand for more than two decades, but it cannot be said that the results are very encouraging.[2] Although there

[2] For a brief survey of recent political developments in Thailand, see John Coast, *Some Aspects of Siamese Politics*, New York: IPR, 1953.

have from time to time been swings in a more liberal direction, the general trend has been toward an authoritarian regime, dominated by a relatively small group of insiders and with an increasingly large role for the military. This latter aspect is one which is particularly disturbing in its implications for neighboring countries in view of the decisive part which the military have come to play in a number of countries of Latin America and the Middle East. As an independent state Thailand was equipped from the outset with its own national armed forces which were brought to an approximation of modernity as a part of the general overhauling of the Siamese state structure. The colonial countries were obviously excluded from the possession of similar national forces, but as soon as they achieved independence (or even substantially earlier, both under and against the Japanese) they undertook the construction of their own military establishments as one of the necessary, if highly unfortunate, attributes of sovereignty. Acting either on their own, or as the instrument drawn upon by the ruling elite to suppress a popular rising or to bolster one faction of the elite against another, the military can obviously become the determining element in political life, putting an end to representative institutions save as the facade behind which the real power is exercised.

The turn away from monarchical absolutism came in Thailand with the revolution of 1932. This revolution, which was in fact more of the order of a speedy and bloodless coup d'état, was distinguished by three features which gave it its special character and largely determined the future course of events.

In the first place, it was conceived and executed by the small Western-educated group which had emerged as a planned part of the modernization of the Siamese state and of some of the upper brackets of Siamese society undertaken by King Chulalongkorn and his successors. Since this group was denied access to power by the principle of absolutism and even more by the monopolistic claims of the royal princes to all the upper offices of state, it was inevitable that they should at some point make a bid for a place in the sun as similar groups regularly have elsewhere. The effects of the economic depression gave them an opportunity to capitalize on other sources of disaffection and to push aside both the princes and the king, who was himself by no means wholly opposed to the adoption of a constitutional system.

Secondly, this group associated with itself and called to its aid some of the military leaders who had likewise been educated abroad. These men, with the armed forces behind them, played a vital role in putting the revolution across and ensuring its success. It has been suggested that the leading officers who were involved in the coup not only quickly learned how easily they could manipulate power but also soon discovered that they could get along quite nicely without the backing of the civilian liberals who had originally drawn them into the plot whereas the latter were too powerless to govern without armed support. From being an instrument for liberal reform the armed forces soon became political actors on their own account.

Thirdly—and this was one of the prime conditions of the ease of military manipulation—it was a revolution which had virtually nothing in the way of popular roots and was in no sense a response to or a result of popular pressures or demands. It was made from on high without mass participation and can actually be seen as bringing about not much more than a substitution of a somewhat larger governing elite of a new type for the traditional smaller one. Despite occasional general elections and some spread of education it has continued to be the fact ever since 1932 that the people at large have shown no wide or stable interest in the political affairs of the country and that changes in government have been the work of insiders rather than—save by accident—the expression of the will of the people. Sir Josiah Crosby concludes that in the actual circumstances liberalism never had a chance to take over a continuing lead:[3]

"Looking back upon the past, it is now easy for the impartial observer to see that the democratic revolution of June, 1932, lacking as it did the basis of any valid public opinion, was doomed to failure from the very start. The moral to be drawn from what happened afterwards is that in any country where the traditional form of government has been weakened or destroyed, and where there is no effective public opinion to supplement or replace it, the existence of relatively powerful Armed Forces must represent a standing menace to the growth of democratic institutions."

The intention of the sponsors of the revolution seems clearly to have been to move gradually toward the introduction of a real democracy. The constitution which was adopted at the outset provided for an assembly which was to be half elected and half appointed, moving at a later stage toward full election when more political experience had been gained and mass education had made greater headway. In the last two decades, as the result of the war and a series of further coups d'état, which have unfortunately shown an increasing trend toward bloodshed, there have been several changes in constitution, the most recent (1951) bringing about a reversion to the 1932 model with an assembly which is in fact completely dominated by the military and their supporters. Civilian rule has flourished at its not overly democratic best during the years from 1934 to 1938 and again in the immediate aftermath of the war until November 1947, when the military once more began to move into power after the stigma of collaboration with the Japanese had lost its force. For the rest of the time

[3] Sir Josiah Crosby, *Siam*, London, 1945, pp. 90–91.

CONCLUSION

since 1932 it has been primarily the military who have been able to dictate the political fortunes of the country.

At least symbolically, if not always in the actual fact of holding power in their own hands, the two principal factions among the so-called promoters of the 1932 revolution —the civilian and the military—have been headed by Nai Pridi Phanemyong (also known by his title, Luang Pradit Manudharm), a brilliant Paris-trained lawyer with leftward leanings, and Luang Pibun Songgram, an Army leader who also secured his military education in France. Power has tended to alternate between these two men or persons put forward by them, although in the years preceding the war there was a period of collaboration between them. In the latest phase, after the coups which brought the military back into the saddle, Pibun has headed several governments in which the military seem to have full sway and the major disturbances of the political calm have come from disagreements between different factions of the armed forces or their leaders. Whether he is himself now a central focal point of power, retains his position by adroit manipulation of opposing cliques within the armed forces, or is essentially no more than the front man for the actual wielders of power remains currently a matter of dispute. Following Pibun's renewed rise, Pridi disappeared to unknown parts, emerging again in mid-1954 in Communist China to charge the existing Thai government with being a tool of the Western imperialists. There remains the possibility that in the uncertainties created by the outcome of the Geneva Conference he will again make a bid for power, perhaps under explicit Communist auspices and with the goal of achieving a new and larger union of Thai people which would embrace parts of South China, Indochina, and Burma as well as Thailand itself.

As in other Southeast Asian countries political parties, when they have been allowed to exist, have tended to center about the leading personalities and have played a lesser role than in the Philippines or Indonesia. At no time have they reached significantly down into the general populace, and Bangkok remains the one effective center of political life. Particularly in the postwar years corruption in the highest places has become an almost institutionalized feature of the Thai governmental system, and the major sources of illicit revenue, including the opium traffic, appear to have been deliberately distributed in such fashion as to hold different interests and leading personages in line. One of the principal starting points of the present wave of corruption was the huge profits opened up in the rice trade when national and international controls were placed on that scarce and vital commodity at the end of the war.

An authoritarian regime, resting on armed force, controlled by military leaders, and deeply scarred with corruption, is a far cry from the democratic and progressive regime which at least some of the civilian leaders had set as the goal for the revolution of 1932—but there is no evidence of any serious popular disaffection. As Southeast Asian standards go, the people are reasonably well-off and the intrigues and reshuffles in the upper political and military circles of Bangkok normally infringe on their lives only remotely, if at all. The large contingent of Chinese in the country, who continue to monopolize or dominate many occupations and trades, are frequently harassed by the nationalist aspirations of the government to replace them by Siamese, but inertia, corruption, and inefficiency combine to give them in fact much more leeway than appears on the surface of the official laws and regulations.[4] Communism, which has a lesser hold in Thailand than in any of the neighboring countries, is almost wholly confined to the Chinese community and is currently no menace to the existing order.

[4] See Richard J. Coughlin, "The Status of the Chinese Minority in Thailand," *Pacific Affairs*, Dec. 1952.

CONCLUSION

This state of affairs forces consideration of a question which should not be ignored even though no certain answer is available. Does the acceptance of the Thai people go beyond a passive acquiescence in a government which has been thrust upon them and whose dictates they fatalistically accept or evade, or is it a type of government which in net effect they find more palatable than they would find an efficient, modern, constitutional system? While the latter might do far better in guaranteeing the observance of rights and procedures, it would also be far more distant from traditional patterns and would in all probability impinge much more on everyday life. Certainly there has up to this point been no significant demand for a popular share in the governmental process: if there had been, the present regime must have been found intolerable and could hardly have survived. Perhaps steps should be taken to instill a "divine discontent" which would build up an irresistible pressure for a new and truly representative order, but as things now stand there is no reason to assume that the popular will has been cheated of its desires, nor can it be taken for granted that change would bring any greater measure of present contentment. This is not to assert that the government has any deep roots in the affection of the people, which seems improbable, but merely that it is a government which is perhaps not out of line with Thai notions of the proper order of things.

It is to be doubted that the Western powers have been much swayed by this line of argument in taking Thailand to their bosom in recent years. The apparent stability of the regime and its ardent anti-Communism have presumably been the determining factors even though this has meant the endorsement of a clearly undemocratic and illiberal government. As a member of the United Nations Thailand has not only been made the seat of the Far Eastern branches of several international organizations and conferences but has also participated actively in the Korean war, and in general has aligned itself firmly with the West. Despite its present leanings, however, it must be open to the gravest question whether Thailand offers a firm point of support for Western policy in Southeast Asia. It is a country which has, for wholly understandable reasons, followed a shifting course, bending and turning with the international breezes, of which the two most recent samples were the wartime alliance with Japan and the postwar turn to the West. The Pibun government rests upon a very slim foundation of active popular support, and it seems only plausible to assume that if Communism should come to look like the wave of the future the government would either be swept away by revolutionary forces or would discover means of making its peace with the new elements.

If we knew with a greater degree of certainty the conditions which are necessary for the success of representative institutions, their prospects in the several Southeast Asian countries could be foretold with reasonable accuracy. The objective social and economic circumstances of these countries are familiar enough in their broad outlines to make summary judgments possible, but it is far more difficult to weigh and evaluate the bearing of the subjective elements. The case of Thailand suggests that the Thai people have no very widespread and urgent desire to make liberal democracy work, and even though the other peoples of the area, because of their colonial background or for other reasons, may have a larger measure of political consciousness we have relatively little knowledge of the extent and depth of the popular demand for the representative institutions with which they are being endowed. Perhaps even more significantly, we have virtually no knowledge of the effective relevance of such demands when whatever may be the necessary objective conditions are lacking. It is perhaps true that where there is no real and deep popular desire for the maintenance of representative government it will before long crumble away, but is the desire itself, assuming it to exist, enough to set the machinery in motion and keep it running?

Objectively, as has been stressed at several points, there are very substantial differences between the social-economic setting in which the experiment of representative government is being undertaken in Southeast Asia and that in which it grew up in Western Europe and the countries settled from Western Europe. Continued economic development on modern lines and the spread of a Western type of education will undoubtedly work to cut down the differences but the rate of change may well be slow, hesitant, and spotty. On the basis of the experience of the last two decades in the Philippines and even more markedly in Thailand it appears justified to conclude that if representative institutions are to have any real significance for Southeast Asia there must be a decided broadening of the political base, at least in the form of a larger indigenous middle class which is both politically aware and politically active. Without the appearance of such a middle class, which has played so large a role elsewhere, or the coming to political maturity of wide segments of the general populace, it is difficult to see how a democratic system can be expected to stand up against the pressures which are already very much in evidence.

In this connection one significant point which deserves close and continued observation is the extent to which Westernization, if this term may be used to indicate the whole trend toward a breach with the traditional past, will find adequate reflection in other than the capital and a few main urban centers. The attraction of these centers for the rising elite and the newly educated is obviously very great, and the demands of the central governmental services and the headquarters of major economic institutions are immense when measured against the available trained manpower. It is by no means difficult to foresee a situation in which there will be a constant drain away from the provinces and the more rural areas of sufficient magnitude seriously to delay their progress and to make of them a stagnant hinterland which the "enlightened" center would administer with greater or less benevolence as the case might be. Instead of encouraging control by the elected representatives of the people and the development of true local self-government, the temptation will be large to achieve at least the appearance of speedier advance by sending out officials from the capital who will administer from above without concerning themselves to secure effective local participation. In every country serious study deserves to be made of these several elements: the draining off of elites to metropolitan centers, the extension of central services and departments at the expenses of local initiative and collaboration, and the smothering of the vitality of the institutions of local government.

It would be absurd to pretend that there are any easy answers in a situation which is snarled with complexity at almost every turning. In Indonesia, for example, there has been an effort to shift away from an over-centralized system of local government with officials appointed from the center to a system of local election which would give a greater degree of expression to the actual needs and desires of the people. This is obviously a development which points in the right direction, but there can also be no doubt that in Indonesia as elsewhere a vast amount of stimulation and direction from the center is needed if any adequate tempo of advance is to be achieved and maintained. While recognizing that the most fundamental condition for lasting and meaningful advance is the winning of the active understanding and participation of the people concerned, one should not ignore that there is likely to be a real danger, at least in the early stages, in having to submit new and complex programs to any detailed approval or control by a local electorate which cannot be assumed to have the information and experience on which intelligent decisions can be based. This is a problem which is universal in the contemporary world where the powers of the scientist and the expert have so far outraced the comprehension of the layman, but it is peculiarly acute in countries where the mass of the population is still illiterate and not far removed from the immemorial ways of its remote ancestors. Inadequate systems of communications and transport, widely scattered populations, and a host of small isolated villages all work to render more difficult the proper balance and flow between the center and the extremities.

In such circumstances the appeal of the several avenues which offer an easy escape from freedom is certain to be great. Of these avenues it is Communism which comes with the largest measure of prestige and the strongest backing from outside; but it remains a striking fact that it is so far the liberal democracy of the West which has carried the day. Although there is likely to be a presumption of strong Socialist leanings and, at least in the cases of Burma and Indonesia, an insistence on neutralism in foreign policy, the domestic political systems are aimed at an approximation of Western Europe and North America and not of Moscow and the people's democracies. How long this line can be held remains to be seen because the attractions which Communism has to offer are very real. It comes equipped not only with the conspiratorial devotion and the organizational and tactical skill of the party leaders and members, but also with the slogans of peace, democracy, and progress. Behind it there stands the success of the Soviet Union, its new empire clustered about it, as one of the two super-powers of the contemporary international scene. The addition of China to the Soviet bloc is at once a further addition to the prestige of Communism and, in the eyes of Southeast Asians, a danger signal because of the nationalist antipathy to the Chinese in the area and the fear of a Chinese imperialist advance under the symbols of hammer and sickle. However much the policies and actions of the Soviet Union may be regarded as retrograde in the West, to many in Southeast Asia they must appear to offer a proved and dynamic answer to their desire to catch up with the advanced countries. To many Asians Communism is an alternative form of Westernization, a forced-draught means of driving forward into the modern world, and it is not the least of the Soviet Union's charms that it presents itself as the overt and most implacable enemy of capitalism and of the Western powers whose imperialism is by no means a forgotten menace.

Yet up to this time it is only in Indochina that Communism has scored any really spectacular gains. In the Philippines the Huks have been able to capitalize on deep-rooted agrarian and other discontents but their strength appears to have declined and they constitute no major threat to the existence of the Philippine government. In Indonesia the Communists' one serious effort at revolution met with defeat at the hands of the Indonesian Republic, and although they have a strong hold in the labor movement they seem to be far from taking over power. Against the Burmese Communists of different denominations the government has been able slowly to assert its unifying force, and in Malaya, despite the loss of life and property inflicted by the guerrillas, Communism has essentially been confined to a small segment of the Chinese population. At least as far as any surface manifestations go, Communism in Thailand has likewise been mainly a Chinese phenomenon and has a lesser hold than in any of the other countries.

In Indochina, on the other hand, Communism continues to be a very real and active threat. There alone, under the leadership of Ho Chi Minh and the Vietminh, it has been able to identify itself with the nationalist movement and establish a regime strong enough and popular enough to hold a large part of the country against the attacks of the French forces and their Vietnamese contingents. Whether

CONCLUSION

Ho and his associates might in the immediate postwar years have been led to adopt a more purely nationalist and less Moscow-oriented position, as many people then thought, has by now become a matter of academic speculation: since 1949–50 the alignment with the Soviet bloc has been thoroughly consolidated and there seems no reason to question the completeness of Communist control in the Vietminh-People's Republic of Vietnam. There is, of course, always the possibility of Titoist defection under proper circumstances, but the events of the last few years hold out scanty hope for such a turn. For any purposes of present policy formulation it is by far the wiser course to assume that the Vietminh is Communist and within the Communist bloc, although this of course does not mean that efforts should be abandoned to drive a wedge between the two partners. The extent of the Vietminh's reliance on Communist China in the course of the Geneva Conference and its apparent readiness to allow the latter to speak for it does not lend encouragement to any belief that a breach between the two is imminent.

In terms of representative government the history of Indochina from the beginning of the French occupation to the present has little to offer. The French colonial pattern in the prewar decades was one of government from the top down rather than from the bottom up, and slight attention was paid to the problem of securing anything approaching an adequate representation of Indochinese opinion. Councils were established at various levels and for various purposes, the most significant being in the colony of Cochinchina, but they were normally endowed with little power, were appointive rather than elective, and, where the elective element entered in, were based on a very limited franchise which heavily favored the French citizens. In consequence, there was only the slimmest opportunity for the Indochinese either to gain political experience or to find openings for the legitimate expression of their political ambitions, and the repressive policies of the French left small room for the formation of political parties. In the administrative services similarly, Indochinese were normally appointed only at the lower levels, Frenchmen being imported to fill many posts which in the colonies of other powers were usually filled by natives of the colony itself. These policies of the French, combined with a restrictive economic system which tied Indochina very closely to France, provided at least some part of the explanation of the constant trend toward a leftward movement in Indochinese political life.

The survival of the French regime in Indochina under Japanese auspices during the bulk of the second World War meant that the Indochinese were denied even the limited experience of a measure of self-government which the Japanese occupation gave the other peoples of Southeast Asia. When the French were pushed aside by the Japanese early in 1945 a coalition of parties with Ho Chi Minh at its head emerged as the principal political force in Vietnam. It was this coalition, comprising not only the Communists but a number of other nationalists and revolutionary groups as well, which declared the independence of the Republic of Vietnam on the surrender of the Japanese and shortly established itself as the actual government of much of the country. Under the aegis of the Republic the first general election in the history of Indochina was held in January 1946, to create a national assembly which later in the year adopted a constitution providing for a bill of rights, a president, and a cabinet responsible to a unicameral legislature to be elected by universal suffrage. This election, conducted under the most difficult conditions, has been both proclaimed as a striking demonstration of the democratic character of the Vietminh and denounced as a largely fraudulent piece of Communist political manipulation.[5] What the later developments might have been under other and happier circumstances is a matter on which there is the widest divergence of opinion. The actual turn of events since the wide-open breach with France after the Vietminh rising in Hanoi, the taking over of China by the Communists, and the tightening of the international lines after the outbreak of the Korean war has been a progressively greater and more overt Communist control which has inevitably meant that the democratic institutions have become more facade than working reality.

The Communist Party itself has gone through several transformations, even including its formal dissolution in November 1945 to meet tactical or strategic needs of the moment, but it appears never to have vanished from the scene or to have surrendered its factual control. In its most recent guise it re-appeared as the Viet-Nam Dang Lao Dong (Vietnam Workers Party) in 1951 with Ho Chi Minh as its president. Through a series of interlocking directorates and the placing of its leaders in a number of key positions it is able to maintain effective control of the government, the armed forces, and the various non-Communist organizations which continue to survive. By the terms of the constitution the national assembly should have a central role in the conduct of the government, but the assembly is said not to have met since the adoption of the constitution, its place being taken by a permanent committee which operates in close accord with the executive. In a number of respects both the party and the government closely resemble the patterns established in the Soviet Union with some features which have been drawn from the variants introduced by the Communists in China.

[5] See, for example, Nguyen Duy Thanh, *My Four Years With the Viet Minh*, Bombay: Democratic Research Service, no date. A former official in the Ho regime, Nguyen Duy Thanh also contends that the fact that non-Communists held high posts in the government was essentially meaningless since all real power was exercised by Communists who were strategically planted in controlling positions.

In view of the paucity of the materials available on the structure and functioning of the Vietminh—properly the Democratic Republic of Vietnam—it may be useful at this point to cite at some length the conclusions arrived at by a young French scholar, Bernard B. Fall, who had an opportunity to undertake an extensive examination on the spot in Vietnam during 1953.

"In its own curious way, the Democratic Republic seems to practise the Marxist principle of the 'withering-away of the state' by replacing or capping state organs by a party machinery that frequently is far more complex and comprehensive than the administrative or executive organ which it parallels. . . .

"After a hopeful beginning of constitutional democratic government, a single party gained control of the state apparatus, the armed forces, and the bulk of the local administrative machinery. This party—a direct successor of the Indochinese Communist Party—has successfully consolidated its grip upon the State so that today the acts and policies of the Democratic Republic closely resemble those of any other state of the Soviet orbit. This does not mean that the Democratic Republic has abandoned its national objectives, particularly as regards its regional aim of supremacy over the other member states of the former Indochinese Federation.

"It cannot be denied that the Viet-Minh—as it is inaccurately called—has long since passed the stage of a 'guerilla government' which many Western sources still think it is. Despite gravest odds, it fulfills all the prerogatives of organized government—including, indeed, a plethora of bureaucratism—over an area of more than 100,000 square miles, and has been recognized by several members of the community of nations.

"Thus, the D.R.V.N. is a State—but a totalitarian state, for by no stretch of the imagination can the regime that at present rules the Republican zone be called 'democratic' in the sense generally attributed to the term, unless autocritiques, 'brain-washing', show trials, supremacy of

CONCLUSION 175

a political party over the governmental machinery, are accepted as part of the system.

"Yet, it is true that the Ho Chi Minh government commands the obedience, if not the affectionate loyalty, of the majority of the Vietnamese."[6]

In the French-controlled areas representative government has been largely conspicuous by its absence, although both Cambodia and Laos have been endowed with elected national assemblies. The situation in the Vietnamese government headed by Bao Dai was summed up by Mr. Justice Douglas in the following terms:[7]

"He has a cabinet whose members have titles that are reminiscent of a republic—Prime Minister or President, Minister of Foreign Affairs, Minister of Education, and the like. But these men are his personal agents. Bao Dai governs by decree. There is no parliament or assembly elected by the people. There is no public forum where the people may air their grievances and enact laws to remedy them. Bao Dai is the repository of all law and all the authority in the land."

Despite protestations of future democratic intent, the steps which the Bao Dai regime has taken toward representative institutions have been few and faltering, but its hesitations, given the realities of its precarious situation, have been thoroughly understandable. Trapped between

[6] Bernard B. Fall, *The Viet-Minh Regime: Government and Administration in the Democratic Republic of Vietnam*, N.Y.: I.P.R. 1954, pp. 41, 116–18. This volume includes the text of the Vietminh Constitution as an appendix.

[7] W. O. Douglas, *North from Malaya*, New York, 1953, p. 196. Another recent American visitor to Indochina, Adlai Stevenson, has also expressed vigorous doubt as to the wisdom and success of French policy in Vietnam, suggesting among other things that free elections should be held to give substance to Vietnam's democratic intentions and start the process of developing responsible leadership. He also comments: "Today in Indochina, the French are too often behaving as in the colonial past: occupying the big palaces, commanding the police and the army, censoring the press." "Ballots and Bullets," *Look*, June 2, 1953.

the French on one side and the Vietnamese nationalists on the other, with the Vietminh always hovering ominously in the background, Bao Dai has had relatively little room for maneuver and any move in a nationalist direction would have been attended by the gravest risks. Only if he were prepared to advocate so intransigent a nationalist policy as to alienate French support could he appeal to the Vietnamese people without the probability of repudiation by them. In these circumstances the only elections on a national basis which his several successive governments have been venturesome enough to hold were those of January 1953 for municipal and communal councils, which, it was suggested, might at some later and more peaceful time serve as the electoral base for regional and national assemblies. These elections produced a relatively large turnout of those eligible to vote, already a somewhat restricted list, but there were great areas of the country under Vietminh control to which no effort was made to extend the balloting. Because of the local character of the electoral campaigns and the absence of both political parties and a free press, it is difficult to secure a clear assessment of the political significance of these elections, but their results appear to have been generally taken as a rebuke to the government of Premier Nguyen Van Tam and a demonstration of nationalist sentiment which was not prepared to accept Bao Dai and his French attachment as satisfying the demand for unity and independence.

At the center the only approximation of a continuing representative body which has been established is a Provisional Consultative Assembly, advisory to Bao Dai as Chief of State and appointed by him to represent different elements of the public. The difficulties which confront the ex-Emperor in any attempt to secure a broader popular base for his regime were brought into the spotlight by the events of the autumn of 1953 when preparations were underway for the negotiation of a new agreement with

France. Early in September an unofficial congress was organized by some trade union and other leaders which put forward demands for unconditional independence, the calling of a national assembly, and a number of other reforms. Perhaps spurred on by this demonstration of the public temper, Bao Dai in October called into being a national congress which was to meet for two days to name twenty men from whom he could pick six to join in the French negotiations. Although it was hand-picked, this congress immediately got out of hand, refused to accept the limits of time and function placed on it, and, to the distinct pain of the French authorities, protested continued membership in the French Union, at least as at present constituted. Not long after these events Nguyen Van Tam vanished from the scene and in January 1954 was succeeded as Premier by Prince Buu Loc who formed an essentially non-political cabinet of experts and technicians. The promises of political reform made by the new premier, who appeared to have little popular hold, were again met by the insistence of political leaders on the summoning of a national assembly which would have authority to pass on any accord with France and undertake immediate preparations for national elections. In June 1954 Prince Buu Loc was replaced as Premier by Ngo Dinh Diem, a Catholic leader represented as having the backing of the United States, on whom fell the unhappy burden of implementing the decisions of the Geneva Conference for his truncated country.[8]

From the available accounts it appears that the administrative structure of Vietnam left almost as much to be desired as did the meager installments of representative government. Although there was some measure of

[8] The minor success and major failures of Bao Dai's Vietnam in the establishment of democratic institutions are reviewed by Bernard B. Fall in "Representative Government in the State of Vietnam," *Far Eastern Survey*, August 1954.

devolution down to the three provinces into which the country was divided prior to the Geneva Conference, it was a regime which, on the customary French model, was over-centralized. Lacking any established popular base, power flowed downward from Bao Dai, and the cabinet, which has been removed and reorganized several times since the ex-Emperor was restored to authority, was made directly responsible to him. Much of the administrative set-up was established on an *ad hoc* basis and has been subject to sporadic change, with the result of considerable confusion, overlapping, and lack of coordination. To an even greater degree than in neighboring countries there has been a marked dearth of capable civil servants, both because the prewar French colonial system had given little scope to Indochinese in the upper and even the middle brackets of the service and because the Vietminh has either attracted men who might otherwise have taken office or has frightened them off by threats of reprisals if they joined the Bao Dai regime. Particularly at the very top for cabinet and near-cabinet posts Bao Dai has found it exceedingly difficult to persuade men of stature to serve because of their disinclination to be identified with a regime so closely associated with the French, so dubiously representative of the Vietnamese national movement, and with so uncertain a claim upon the future. For this and a number of other reasons, including the war situation and the reluctance of France to surrender control, many French officials continued to occupy positions in the government, thus casting further doubt on the qualified independence which had been granted.

The situation created by the French military defeats in Indochina and the agreements hammered out at Geneva contains basically new elements of outstanding importance but the events and attitudes of the past, both recent and more remote, will inevitably continue to cast their shadow before them. On the model of Korea, but with differences which are at least as great as the similarities, a cease-fire has been achieved which divides the Vietnamese nation in two on approximately the seventeenth parallel. In contrast to Korea this division does not correspond to the fighting lines at the time it came into effect nor do the new north and south Vietnams represent the effective jurisdiction of the existing states at that time, even though it was roughly true that the Vietminh was most strongly consolidated in the north and the French-Bao Dai regime in the south. As against the loose hope that Korea might some day be united, specific provision has been made in the agreements for an election to be held two years hence in the whole of Vietnam to settle the destiny of that country. Although there are many reasons to suspect that this election may never come to pass, its inclusion in the terms of settlement at Geneva will surely serve as a stimulant to the efforts on both sides to win the allegiance of the Vietnamese people. And, to complicate the matter, the states of Cambodia and Laos are confirmed in their separate existence and must consolidate both their domestic affairs and their new relations with the two Vietnams and with France.

On the face of it the advantage seems to lie heavily on the side of the Vietminh in the contest for the allegiance of the Vietnamese. The Geneva Conference outcome represented a very substantial victory for the Vietminh in particular and for the Communist camp in general even though the French were able to secure terms which were more favorable to them in several respects than the balance of military and political power at the moment appeared to make it necessary for the opposing forces to grant. Included among these favorable items was the provision that the Vietnamese election would not be held until after a two year interval as against the prospect of an election coming within a few months after the end of the fighting. If the immediate as opposed to the postponed election had been decided upon, there can be little doubt that the Vietminh would have swept the field.

Virtually all reports concur in the judgment that at least at an earlier stage Ho Chi Minh was the center of the Vietnamese nationalist aspirations, and he has remained, actually or symbolically, a very powerful center of attraction. He and his associates have built up a state which under extraordinarily difficult conditions has not only withstood the attacks of the French, increasingly armed, financed, and backed by the United States, but has been able with Chinese aid to push the French back, inflict serious defeats on them, and to bring them to a position so desperate as to impel Premier Mendès-France to risk his dramatic gamble of achieving a cease-fire within thirty days. In the last four or five years Ho has unquestionably suffered some loss in popular appeal, presumably because of the tightening up of his regime in Communist directions and because of the closeness of his ties with China, but the evidence indicates that those who drifted away from him tended rather to join the ranks of the wavering *attentistes* than to rally around the standards of Bao Dai. Furthermore, despite all the unpleasant and, to Western eyes at least, repulsive features of a Communist society, the Vietminh has carried through land and other reforms of real significance, has acted with vigor and decision, and, perhaps most important of all, has steadfastly and successfully opposed the re-extension of French colonial rule to all of Vietnam.

On the other side, the efforts of the French to counter the appeal of Ho by building up the national stature of Bao Dai and to break the hold of the Vietminh by creating another and "legitimate" Vietnam have met with only very partial success at the best. If Ho has suffered from his association with China (in which country, it should be remembered, Indochinese nationalist movements have regularly taken refuge), Bao Dai must have suffered substantially more from his association with France which left him wide open to the charge of being in fact not much more than a French puppet. Neither reforms nor vigor have characterized his management of the affairs of Vietnam, there have been charges of large-scale corruption against both French and Vietnamese officials, and it was clearly evident that the whole conduct of the war was in French and not Vietnamese hands. The reiterated promises of France to grant full and complete independence to Vietnam always fell far short of actual sovereignty, and the degree to which France retained substantive control was reflected in the apparent readiness of the French negotiators at Geneva to agree to a settlement gravely prejudicial to its proteges with only the scantiest consultation with the Vietnamese leaders established under its and Bao Dai's auspices. That not only the Vietnamese were dissatisfied with the amount of independence accorded them by the French was clearly evidenced by the protests of the King of Cambodia in 1953 and his threats to remove his country from the French Union. Although there have been some signs of a French readiness to rethink the implications of the Union, both Vietnamese and Cambodians have protested against its present unilateral character, seeing it not as an association of equal partners but rather as a French-constructed political instrument by which France continues to control the destinies of the states associated with it.[9]

The Geneva Conference bequeathed immense and extraordinarily difficult problems to Indochina and all the countries concerned with its present and future fate. Aside

[9] For a detailed account of the background of present affairs in Indochina, see Ellen Hammer, *The Struggle for Indochina,* Stanford, 1954. The Cambodian position is examined by Virginia Thompson and Richard Adloff in "Cambodia Moves Toward Independence," *Far Eastern Survey,* Aug. 1953, and three despatches by Tillman Durdin in the *New York Times,* March 8, 9, and 11, 1954. Vietnamese doubts concerning the French Union are elaborated by Nguyen-Dac-Khe, "The Independence of Viet-Nam and the French," *Asia* (Saigon), Sept. 1953, pp. 216–30.

from the immediate difficulties involved in the withdrawal of the armed forces to their designated locations and the movement of civilian populations from one side of the line to the other, there is the need in the Vietnamese territories to reorder state structures in such fashion as to establish effective political control within the newly fixed provisional boundaries and to start the vitally necessary work of reconstructing the country after more than seven years of unrelenting and devastating warfare. A new set of relationships must be created between the four states which now exist in Indochina and between each one of them and the French. On the latter score it is obviously of particular consequence, in view of the proposed future national election, to secure a stable, progressive, and independent government in south Vietnam which can, in the time which lies ahead, serve as a real center of attraction for Vietnamese national sentiment. It remains to be established that a national regime not Communist in inspiration can be set in motion which can stand by itself and meet the desires of the Vietnamese without either the support of French bayonets or French political and economic intervention. Even though a halt has been called to the fighting, it is questionable that south Vietnam can within the immediate future build up an army which could begin to match the Vietminh forces without substantial aid from the French military and the Foreign Legion. If French military forces remain the principal bulwark, real independence is still remote.

For any imperial power as well as for the colony itself, getting out from under a colonial situation is a painful and intricate process. In the particular circumstances of Indochina the colonial system has left a heritage of political and military entanglement which it has proved peculiarly difficult to break through. The leadership of Mendès-France has brought the French government to a recognition of the need to cut its commitments to the measure of its power and potentialities, but it will still be far from easy to cut clean from Indochina not only in terms of French interests but also because of the very real needs of the Indochinese countries themselves and the pressures of the international situation. At Geneva the military phase was brought to an end, but the demand for constructive statesmanship remains at least as great as ever. Far more in the way of political imagination and daring are needed than have been shown up to now, save perhaps in the wise decision that even the harsh verdict of the Geneva Conference was preferable to a continuance of the war in Indochina or its extension into the dread realms of a third world war. The Vietnamese of the south, and the Cambodians and Laotians as well, must be given full access to power in their own affairs, endowed with representative institutions through which the popular will can express itself, and placed in effective charge of the administrative apparatus. Unless steps of this sort are boldly taken by the French it is hard to see what other outcome there can be than continued stalemate and disaffection which can only play into the hands of the Communists. The physical scars of long drawn out colonial and civil war can be more easily erased than the deep bitterness and hostilities which it leaves behind it, and it would be idle to think that there can be any swift movement toward the establishment of smooth-running representative institutions. The Vietnam of Bao Dai gives much evidence of being, in the aftermath of Geneva, a demoralized and discredited regime. To restore it to health and vitality will be a major task.

What is done in Indochina itself is obviously of great moment, but it is by no means impossible that the attitudes and policies adopted by the powers will have an even greater effect. In the last phases of the crisis the United States, Great Britain, Communist China, and the Soviet Union all became very directly and profoundly involved, and the neighboring Asian powers cannot help but have an intense interest in future developments even though they were left largely standing on the sidelines. It was, after all, not in Saigon or Hanoi that the end of the war was achieved but in distant Geneva. It remains to be established that the major opponents in the cold war are in fact prepared to abide honestly by the letter and spirit of the Geneva settlement and to move forward on an agreed and amicable basis toward the building of three independent countries in Indochina which can work out their own salvation without becoming submerged in the global battle of warring ideologies and coalitions.

The Communists have achieved a victory of no small dimensions, but only the event can tell whether they will be content with it for present purposes or merely use their gains as a stepping stone for further advance. A number of different contingencies can be hypothetically foreseen but there is no real evidence on which to base an estimate even of the probabilities. Will the Democratic Republic of Vietnam have an independent sovereignty of its own or will it be forced into the position of a pliant satellite of its great neighbor to the north? If Peking has the imperial ambitions which have been attributed to it in some quarters, the whole of Southeast Asia is obviously in danger and moves to take over Cambodia and Laos and to make impossible the existence of the half of Vietnam which has been left to the free world may be expected in the near future. Direct and open aggression on these countries or on Thailand either by north Vietnam or more flagrantly by China would be relatively easy to meet in the sense that much of world opinion could be mobilized against it, but in the likelier event of internal disturbances which bear at least the color of domestic national uprisings the issues would become far more complex. As the United States found to its surprised pain in the months preceding the cease-fire, there is a large gap between American charges of Communist aggression and Red imperialism and the readiness of other powers to intervene in situations which have the look of popular movements for self-determination, particularly when such intervention runs the risk of precipitating global war. Of the rights and wrongs of democracy in such circumstances there is still much to be explored and evaluated. What is to be the verdict if peoples with apparent freedom use their democratic rights to opt for Communism?

The strident efforts of the administration in Washington in the first half of 1954 to spur the French on to greater martial efforts, to persuade public and Congressional opinion of the need for American intervention, and to build a grand coalition which would give fighting support to the cause of the French and Bao Dai met with rebuffs on almost every side and left the United States isolated and at a very low ebb of diplomatic prestige. Although it gingerly rejoined the last stage of the Geneva Conference it would give no greater immediate support to the agreements that had been achieved than the grudging statement that it would refrain from the threat or use of force to disturb them. Among the outstanding issues which remained was the determination of the kind of guarantee which might be secured to maintain the peace of Southeast Asia and to hold back the threat of further Communist expansion. In its simplest terms the argument revolved around the American drive to get prompt agreement among those states prepared to commit themselves to the containment of Communism as against the British contention that any agreement which failed to include such significant Asian nations as India, Indonesia, and Burma was likely to do more harm than good, to be more provocative than pacifying in a situation already too dangerously aggravated. For the United States the drive to hold back Communism tended always to take precedence over all other concerns, but for many of the other powers this characteristic American view was an over-simplification which they found it impossible to accept.

That Communism has no necessary and fatal attraction for Southeast Asia is evidenced by the fact that the special circumstances of Indochina were required to produce a coalescence of Communism and nationalism, sought for elsewhere in the area by the Communists but nowhere achieved. There is certainly no reason to assume any devotion of the Southeast Asians to the esoteric body of Communist doctrine; but there is, regrettably, equally little reason to assume devotion to the somewhat less articulate and far less precise doctrine of liberal democracy. Both will presumably be judged by their works in practice. Although we can have no certainty as to the criteria of judgment—a study of the expectations and desires of the ordinary human being in Southeast Asia would be of great interest—it seems reasonable to postulate that the two major ones would be the achievement and unimpaired maintenance of national independence and a steady increase in popular well-being.

On the latter score there has in recent years been a widespread assumption that economic development, particularly if broadly interpreted to include social, educational, and administrative reform, will lay the necessary foundations for representative institutions. It may be true that representative government of a modern type needs a firm underpinning of economic development, but the historical record by no means bears out an argument that a liberal democratic system is a necessary, or perhaps even a likely, consequence of such development. The late comers to economic advance—Germany, Russia, and Japan, for example—have been far from furnishing models of representative government, and there is on the face of it no reason to assume that Southeast Asian countries would follow the course of the United States or Britain rather than that of Japan or Russia.

It is certainly an arguable proposition that an increase in economic and social well-being coming to Southeast Asia under the symbols of the West will keep that area from drifting into the domain of Moscow or Peking, but to contend that it will at all necessarily mark out the path to democracy is quite a different story. Indeed, a highly plausible case can be made for the contention that the most direct road to economic development for underdeveloped areas leads by way of an authoritarian rather than a democratic system; and, as has been suggested more than once in this study, there is in Southeast Asia both a predisposition on the part of the mass of the people toward the acceptance of authoritarian direction and, at least not infrequently, a readiness on the part of the leaders to give it. The more insistent the demand for economic advance the greater may be the willingness to yield to authoritarianism's claim to produce speedy results; and the return to the democratic systems which the nationalist leaders now seek to establish may be postponed far beyond the horizon. Of the pressing need of economic development to overcome the backwardness of the area and the dire poverty of most of its people there can be no question, but it should be entered into with eyes open to the uncertainty of its effects on both the national and the international political scene.

Leaving aside these wider and more speculative questions as to the future of representative institutions in Southeast Asia, there is a great deal which remains to be done if we are to have an adequate understanding of their present functioning. Constitutions and the formal framework of government are sufficiently readily available, but to penetrate into the working substance of government in such fashion as to acquire a meaningful comprehension of what actually goes on from day to day and month to month will require much intensive research on the spot. Certainly there can be no easy assumption that because the outward and institutional pattern of political life is modeled on that of familiar systems, therefore the inner processes and relationships represent equally familiar models. What is the actual nature of the parliamentary system in each of the countries where it has been established? What is the role of president and premier, of the cabinet and individual cabinet members, of the parliament as a whole and its committees, of civil servants and experts? To answer these and a host of further questions it would be of immense interest to have a series of case studies in the actual decision-making process, selected in such fashion as to illustrate different facets of the functioning of government in each of the countries.

Such studies obviously should not be confined either to the level of the central government or to the formal political institutions. As the instigators, be they Fascist or Communist, of drives for *Gleichschaltung* well know, the effective maintenance of democracy is dependent upon the existence of a vast number of independent instrumentalities, such as those of local and provincial governments, of political parties, of voluntary societies of many types, of trade unions and other organs of the economic system, and of religious bodies. For the individual citizen to be able to shape his conclusions freely and intelligently there must be a system of mass education and open channels of information and communication. If he is to bring these conclusions to bear significantly upon the decision-making process of government there must be not only free, honest, and regular elections but also associations such as those which have just been suggested through which particular interests, groupings, and viewpoints can find organized and coherent expression. The other side of the coin, equally deserving of study, is the question of the extent to which such pressure groups have been able to manipulate the machinery of government in their own interest.

Although of course each country has its own particular structure and set of problems which require investigation, a few general lines of inquiry may be suggested which should have wide relevance. In the special setting of Southeast Asia the future role of religion and of the religious leaders is likely to be of outstanding importance. Although the religious communities are generally far less compactly organized than those of the West—the Catholic Church in the Philippines is an obvious exception—the hold of the traditional religions is still very strong and penetrates deeply into the spirit and pattern of life of the people. The peculiarly strong influence of Buddhism on postwar Burma has been commented on above as has the significance of Mohammedanism for the political life of Indonesia. Whether overtly or behind the scenes the religious leaders may be able to exercise a large measure of political power and perhaps even play a decisive role not only in the determination of specific governmental policies but also in the evolution of broader trends such as a return to traditionalism or a movement toward a more secular society based on advanced modern technology.

As a possible counterbalancing force close attention should also be given to the development of the trade unions which are peculiarly a manifestation of the newer forces which are operating. Obviously a key point of penetration for the Communists, the unions have also the potentiality of becoming strongholds of democracy in a free society through which the formerly oppressed and exploited can bring immense political influence to bear.

The centrality of political parties for any system of representative institutions makes close observation of their growth in Southeast Asia an inescapable necessity. In the past they have tended to cluster about leading personalities rather than to represent differences of ideology or interest, but if the masses are to be drawn into effective political expression and participation the parties must presumably take on a very different cast. Their structure, the nature and extent of the working democracy within them, and their relation to the processes of government are all matters which should be examined in as much detail as possible. Since the parties are likely to be one of the principal vehicles through which new blood and new elements of the society are drawn into political life it will be highly important to watch over the years where the new leadership is coming from and what encouragement is given to persons representing previously neglected areas and strata of society. It is of equal importance to conduct the same type of inquiry into the structure and composition of the ever-growing administrative hierarchy which must form a highly influential group in states proclaiming social welfare goals.

Another significant but highly difficult field of study concerns the independence of judgment which citizens of Southeast Asian countries may be able to exercise in canvassing political alternatives and particularly in the concrete act of voting. In connection with elections in India and Burma, in Indochina and the Philippines, the cynic (or perhaps the realist) has not infrequently commented that while the democratic forms may have been well observed, the substance was in fact obedience by the mass of the voters to commands or counsels which came to them authoritatively from above. Certainly in the early stages of a democratic system introduced abruptly into a society accustomed to authoritarian decision by traditional leaders there must be a period of growing pains during which the ordinary human being comes to an awareness that he is both able and supposed to make up his own mind. Research into the nature and duration of these growing pains should offer very substantial rewards even though the margin of error would inevitably be large. It should perhaps also be added that any close approach to a realization of the ideals of representative government requires not only independence of mind on the part of the individual citizen but also, on his part and that of his leaders, a strong sense of responsibility. The continued functioning of democracy demands as much wise restraint in the exercise of power as it does readiness to use power to achieve goals which seem of immediate and pressing importance. The demagogue and the totalitarian of the right or the left can be at least as destructive of democracy as the indifferent or the traditionally-minded who make no use of their political prerogatives.

It has been one of the striking features of the colonial age, now in its last throes, that it tended to impose sharp limits on the mutual intercourse of the Asian peoples and to focus the attention of each of them on the West in general or, in the case of actual dependencies, on the particular imperial center. Since the end of World War II and in part through the channels of the United Nations and the specialized agencies there has been a counter-movement to establish a measure of Asian solidarity or at least of close collaboration between some of the Asian states and peoples. South Asia has been the scene of several regional conferences, of which the most recent was the meeting in Colombo in 1954 of India, Pakistan, Burma, Ceylon, and Indonesia to deal with some of the issues surrounding the Indochina crisis and the Geneva Conference. In one fashion or another all Asian countries are confronting similar problems and experiencing similar difficulties as they move into the modern world and seek to establish democratic institutions. There is every reason to assume that through an intensification of relations and deliberate exchange of experience among themselves they could be of very great mutual benefit to each other. Even despite the revolt against colonialism there continues to be too widespread an assumption in Asia as well as in the West that the newly established states should seek guidance and assistance from the United States and Western Europe. It is obvious that the West still has much which it can give, but it seems equally obvious that increasingly there should be intimate collaboration between political leaders, parliamentarians, administrators, journalists, and scholars of the several Asian countries all of which must deal with similar predicaments. It may be that in tactful and unobtrusive fashion such bodies as Unesco and the considerable number of organizations devoted to political science and public administration could be of service as intermediaries in stimulating such regional interchange.

No one should come to the study of Southeast Asian political institutions with the fixed preconception that they should conform to established Western models. At the risk of repetition, let it be said again that these are societies which are in revolution and are seeking to find their own way of life between an old world and a new. Furthermore, it must constantly be kept in mind that democracy, which is the heart of the matter of which representative institutions are only the external and political expression, is by no means only a type of political structure. Far more significantly it is a state of mind and a basic social pattern enabling men to live together in equality and freedom. It rests upon that elusive but fundamental concept of the dignity of the individual human being, and upon an all-pervading sense that the ordinary man of the street and the village has rights which must be respected and values and interests which must be mirrored in the society of which he forms a part. No single political formula can be set up by which to measure whether or not a society reaches the goals implicit in the democratic creed. Ultimate judgment rests not upon conformity to institutional frameworks which have been established elsewhere, but upon the effective ability of the citizen of high or low estate to make his voice heard and to live in the conviction that the government of his society is not a remote and alien enterprise but a living process in which he participates on equal terms. These are things of which Southeast Asia has known little in the past, and toward which it now strives.

Index

AFPFL, *see* Anti-Fascist People's Freedom League
Acheh revolt, 35, 38
Anti-Fascist People's Freedom League (AFPFL), 44–45, 51, 52, 135
Army, Indonesian, controversy over reform, 31–32; role in politics, 33; *see also* Military
Asian-Arab bloc: Burma's role in, 52; Indonesia's role in, 17
Attlee, Clement, 45, 49
Aung San, 44, 45, 51
Avelino, Jose, 105

Ba Swe, U, 53
Bao Dai, 138, 175, 176, 177, 178, 179, 180, 181, 185
Bedale, Harold, 145
Bell Report, Philippines, 101, 104
British Malaya, *see* Malaya
Buddhism, in Burma, 41, 48, 51, 53, 56
Burma: prewar British rule, 41–42; Japanese occupation, 42–43; achievement of independence, 44–45; postwar constitution, 45–49; postwar disturbances, 49–50; elements of stability, 50–52; foreign policy, 52–53; domestic policies, the welfare state, 53–56; local government, 120–21, 123–24, 136–38
Buu Loc, Prince, 177

Cabinet: Burmese, 46; Indonesian, under 1950 constitution, 24–1948 crisis, 25, instability, 26–27, 29, 1953 crisis, 32; in Malaya, steps toward, 67–68, 70, 74
Cambodia, 175, 181
Capitalism, associated with colonialism, 9
Carnell, Francis G., quoted, 81, 88
Catholic Church, in Philippines, 93, 113
Celebes, disturbances in, 38
Ceylonese, in Malaya, 66, 67, 68, 78
China, Communist, 163, 169, 171, 184
China, Nationalist, troops in Burma, 53
Chinese: in Indonesia, 19; in Malaya, 58–91 *passim*, 143; in Philippines, 103; in Southeast Asia, 9; in Thailand, 164
Christianity, *see* Catholic Church
Chulalongkorn, King, 160
Cities, *see* Municipal government
Citizenship problem in Malaya, 84–86
Civil service: in Burma, 135; in Indonesia, 20, 36–38; in Malaya, 88; in Vietnam, 178
Colonialism, influence on political development, 7–9; *see also* France, Great Britain, Netherlands
Communism: in Burma, 44, 45, 49–52, 170; in Indochina, 138, 139–41, 170–75 *passim*, 179–80, 184, 185–86; in Indonesia, 25, 29, 32–33, 34, 35, 38, 170; in Malaya, 59, 62, 76, 79, 80, 82, 83, 84, 88, 90, 170; in Philippines, 102, 114,

Communism (cont'd)
170; in Southeast Asia, 151, 169–70; in Thailand, 164, 170
Constitutions: Burmese, of 1947, 45–49; Indonesian, of 1945, 21–23–of 1950, 23–24; Malayan, 66–68, 74, 77; Philippine, 93–97; Southeast Asian, Western influence on, 5–6, 11; Thai, 162
Crosby, Sir Josiah, quoted, 162
Culture, influence on political development, 10–11

Darul Islam, 33, 34–35, 38
Democratic Party, Philippines, 112, 117
Diem, see Ngo Dinh Diem
Douglas, William O., quoted, 57, 175

Economic influences on political evolution: colonial economy, 8–9; depression of 1930's, 4–5, 19; development programs, 9, 19, 187
Education: in Indonesia, under Dutch regime, 19–20, 37; in Malaya, problem of, 86–87; in Philippines, 93, 111–12
Elections: in Burma, of 1951, 51–52–local, 36; in Indonesia, 1953 electoral law, 27–28–local, 131–32; in Malaya, 68–74, 76, 77–local, 141–43; in Philippines, 105–108, 112–14; in Southeast Asia, 190–91; in Vietnam (French), of 1946, 172–73–of 1953, 175, local, 138–39; in Vietnam (Vietminh), local, 140
Eurasians: in Indonesia, 20, 37; in Malaya, 66, 67, 78
Executive, see President

Fabian Colonial Bureau, quoted, 76
Fall, Bernard B., quoted, 174–75
Federalism: in Burma, 47–48; in Indonesia, 35–36; in Malaya, 63–64

Feith, Herbert, quoted, 27
Foreign enterprise and political development, 8–9
France, policy in Indochina, 171–72, 175–79, 180–83
Furnivall, J. S., quoted, 11; comment on, 42

GAMO, see Groupement Administratif Mobile Opérationnel
Geneva Conference, 163, 171, 177, 178, 179, 181, 183, 184, 185, 191
Great Britain, policy in Burma, 41–
Greater Indonesian Party, 29, 32
Groupement Administratif Mobile Opérationnel (GAMO), 139

Hansard Society, quoted, 13
Hatta, 21, 23, 25, 33
Hayden, Joseph R., 98
Ho Chi Minh, 170, 172, 173, 175, 180
Hukbalahap, 102, 114, 170

IMP, see Independence of Malaya Party
42, 44–45; in Malaya, 58–91
Independence of Malaya Party (IMP), 79, 80, 81, 82, 88
Irian, West, 28
Islam, see Mohammedanism
India: relations with Indonesia, 17; Burma ruled as part of, 42
Indians in Malaya, 59, 60, 61, 62, 66, 67, 72, 77, 78, 82, 86, 91
Indochina, see Cambodia, Laos, Vietnam
Indonesia: prewar Dutch rule, 18–21; postwar conflict with Dutch, 4–5, 17–18, 21; constitutions, of 1945, 21–23–of 1950, 23–24; role of president, 24–26; cabinets, instability, 26–27; electoral law, 28; legislature, 28–29; political parties, 29–31; October 1952 incident and aftermath, 31–33; role of Islam, 33–35; federalism, 35–36; leadership, 36–

INDEX

Indonesia (cont'd)
38; political morale, 38–40; local government, 120–21, 125, 130–35; decentralization of government, 168

Japanese occupation: of Burma, 43; of Malaya, 62; of Southeast Asia, 3–4; of Thailand, 145
Java, Darul Islam in, 34, 38
Jogjakarta, Sultan of, 31, 32, 33

Kahin, George McT., quoted, 20
Khun Lert, 148
Kuala Lumpur, 1952 elections, 81

Labor: in Philippines, 103–104; in Southeast Asia, role in politics, 189
Labour Party, Malaya, see Pan-Malayan Labour Party
Lacson, Arsenio, 111
Landlordism: in Indonesia, lack of, 19; in Philippines, 101–102, 114
Laos, 175
Leadership: in Burma, 41, 45, 56–57; in Indonesia, 19–21, 30, 36–38; in Southeast Asia, 7–8, 11, 155–56; in Vietnam, 178; see also Civil service
Legislatures: Burmese, 46–47; Indonesian, under Dutch regime, 20–21—under 1945 constitution, 23, under 1950 constitution, 24, divorced from public opinion, 27, structure of, 28–29; Malayan legislative councils, 65–75, 76, 77; Philippine, 96–99; Vietnamese, 176–77
Lenin, V. I., 9
Liberal Party, Philippines, 94, 99, 104, 107, 112, 113, 116
Local government: in Burma, 54, 135–38; in Indonesia, 36, 130–35; in Malaya, 141–45; in Philippines, 109–12; in Southeast Asia, prewar, rural, 119–22, 123–29–prewar, municipal, 122–23, 127–28, postwar, 118–19, 129–30; in Thailand, 145–49; in Vietnam, 138–41
Lubis, Mochtar, quoted, 31
Lyttelton, Oliver, 73, 89

MCA, see Malayan Chinese Association
Madiun revolt, 25, 33
Magsaysay, Ramon, 102, 105, 107–109, 113–16, 159
Malaya: communal problem, 58–61; British prewar policies, 61–62; Japanese occupation, 62; postwar political reorganization, 63–64; slow growth of democratic institutions, 64–65; postwar constitutions, 66–68; development of elected councils, 68–70; proposals for further development, 70–74; Rendel proposals for Singapore, 74–75; arguments for extending elective principle, 76–77; conduct of elections, 77–78; political parties, 78–83; government policy toward Chinese and Malays, 83–84; question of non-Malay citizenship, 84–86; educational problem, 86–87; current problems, 86–91; local government, 120–21, 122, 127–28, 141–45
Malayan Chinese Association (MCA), 70–73, 79–81, 82, 83
Mangkorn Promyothi, General, 149
Masjumi, 27, 29, 30, 32, 34–35, 131
Mendès-France, Pierre, 180
Middle class: in Philippines, 103–107; in Southeast Asia, lack of indigenous, 9–10; political role, 167
Military role in politics: in Indonesia, 31–33; in Thailand, 160–63
Minorities: in Burma, 46–48, 50, 52; see also Ceylonese, Chinese, Eurasians, Indians

Mohammedanism in Indonesia, 17; controversy over Islamic state, 34–35; *see also* Darul Islam, Masjumi
Moluccas, disturbances in, 38
Moslems, *see* Mohammedanism
Municipal government: in Burma, 122–23; in Indonesia, 134; in Malaya, 63, 66, 74, 75, 127–28, 141–43; in Philippines, 110–11; in Southeast Asia, 122; in Thailand, 127, 148–49

Nacionalista Party, Philippines, 94, 99, 100, 104, 105, 107, 108, 109, 112, 115–16, 117
Nationalist Party, Indonesia (PNI), 27, 29, 32–33, 34, 35, 131
Natsir, 27, 35, 131
Negara Party, Malaya, 82
Netherlands, policy in Indonesia, prewar, 18–21; postwar, 17–18, 21
New Guinea, *see* Irian
New Statesman and Nation, quoted, 89
Ngo Dinh Diem, 177
Nguyen Van Tam, 138, 176, 177
Nu, U (Thakin Nu), 45, 51, 53, 54

Onn bin Jaafar, Dato, 79, 80, 144
Osmena, Sergio, 94, 100

PNI, *see* Nationalist Party, Indonesia
PVO, *see* People's Volunteer Organization
Pan-Malayan Labour Party, 72, 73, 78, 81, 82
Pantjasila (Five Principles), 22
Partai Nasional Indonesia, *see* Nationalist Party, Indonesia
People's Volunteer Organization (PVO), Burma, 49
Persetuan Indonesia Raya, *see* Greater Indonesian Party
Philippines: historical background, 92–93; constitution, 93–94; role of president, 11, 94–97; role of legislature, 96–99; political parties, 99–101, 104; peasant problems, 101–103; middle class, 103; labor, 103–04; elections, 105–109; local government, 109–12; Magsaysay administration, 112–17; political progress evaluated, 158–59; Communism in, 170
Pibun Songgram, 147, 163, 166
Plural society: in Burma, 42; in Malaya, 59, 61
Political parties: Burmese, 42, 44–45, 49, 51, 52, 135; Indonesian, 27, 29–35 *passim*, 38, 131, 133; Malayan, 70–74, 78–83, 88; Philippine, 94, 99–102, 104, 105, 107–109 *passim*, 112–17 *passim*, 170; Southeast Asian, 189–90; Thai, 163–64
President: in Burma, 46–47; in Indonesia, constitutional powers, 22–24—Sukarno's role, 24–26, *see also* Sukarno; in Philippines, 94–97
Pridi Phanemyong, 147, 163
Progressive Party, Malaya, 78
Proportional representation in Indonesia, 28
Purcell, Victor, quoted, 70, 86
Pyidawtha movement, 54–56, 136

Quezon, Manuel, 94, 95, 96, 100, 110, 159
Quirino, Elpidio, 104, 107, 110, 113

RIDA, *see* Rural and Industrial Development Authority
Recto, Claro, 116
Regionalism, 191
Religion, role in politics, 189; *see also* Buddhism, Catholic Church, Mohammedanism
Rendel, Sir George, 74–75
Representative institutions, problem of definition, 13–14

Research on Southeast Asia, need for, 187
Romulo, Carlos, 112, 117
Roxas, Manuel, 94, 96
Rural and Industrial Development Authority (RIDA), Malaya, 141, 144

Sastroamidjojo, Ali, 32, 33
Singapore, government of, 63, 66, 74, 75, 141–42
Sjahrir, 23, 25, 32
Sjarifuddin, Amir, 25, 33
Socialism: in Burma, 41, 48–49, 52, 53; in Indonesia, 29, 32; proposed for Malaya, 89
Socialist Party, Indonesia, 29, 32
Sukarno, 21, 22, 23, 24–26, 32, 33, 34, 155; quoted, 38–39
Sukiman, 27
Sumatra, Acheh revolt, 35, 38
Sumulong, Juan, 100

Tam, see Nguyen Van Tam
Tan, Sir Cheng-lock, 73, 80
Taruc, Luis, 114
Templer, General Sir Gerald, 68, 70, 83, 88; quoted, 69
Thailand: local government, 118, 121, 126–27, 145–49; military role in politics, 160–63; 1932 revolution, 160–62; constitutions, 162; political parties, 163–64; political system evaluated, 164–66
Than Tun, 44
Times (London), quoted, 82–83

UMNO, see United Malays National Organization
Unesco, 192
United Malays National Organization (UMNO), 70–73, 79–81, 82, 83
United Nations: Burma's role in, 52; Indonesia's role in, 17
United States, foreign relations: Burma, 53; Indochina, 185–86; Philippines, 115

Vietnam: local government, French regime, 120–21, 124–25, 138–41 —Vietminh regime, 139–41; prewar French policy, 171–72; Vietminh policies, 173–75, 179–80; Bao Dai government, 175–81; situation in 1954, 181–85

Western influence on political development, 5–6, 11, 19, 153–54, 167–68
Wilopo, 27, 32
Wongsonegoro, Dr., 32
World War II, effects on political development, 3–4

DUE

DARTMOUTH COLLEGE
3 3311 00528 8594